W9-AFI-930

God's Perfect Plan

for Imperfect People

God's Perfect Plan
for Imperfect People
The Message of Ephesians

Thomas A. Jones
Foreword by Henry Kriete

DPI
DISCIPLESHIP
PUBLICATIONS
INTERNATIONAL

God's Perfect Plan for Imperfect People

© 2001 by Discipleship Publications International
2 Sterling Road, Billerica, Mass. 01862-2595

All rights reserved. No part of this book may be duplicated, copied, translated, reproduced or stored mechanically or electronically without specific, written permission of Discipleship Publications International.

Printed in the United States of America

All Scripture quotations, unless indicated, are taken from the HOLY BIBLE, NEW INTERNATIONAL VERSION. Copyright © 1973, 1978, 1984 by the International Bible Society. Used by permission of Zondervan Publishing House. All rights reserved.

The "NIV" and "New International Version" trademarks are registered in the United States Patent Trademark Office by the International Bible Society. Use of either trademark requires the permission of the International Bible Society.

"Additional Notes" prepared by Mike Van Auken and used by permission.

ISBN: 1-57782-136-X

Cover Design: Tony Bonazzi
Interior Design: Corey Fisher

*To the elders and evangelists and their wives in the
Northwest region of the Boston church,
I love you all.
It is an honor to serve with you. May God help us
work and love together and build the kind of church
described in the Letter to the Ephesians.*

Contents

Foreword

One of the most dramatic images of our salvation found anywhere in the Scriptures is in Ephesians 2:1-10. We were, to put it bluntly, dead in our sins—completely powerless, utterly helpless, entirely unable to do anything to save ourselves. Not only had our sins defeated us, but they had also engulfed and buried us. And here, in these tombs, in this graveyard of darkness, we were without hope and without God. Even more frightening, Paul says we were by nature objects of wrath. This is a grim picture.

Then something wonderful happened. "But because of his great love for us, God, who is rich in mercy, made us alive with Christ even when we were dead in transgressions" (Ephesians 2:4-5). Just try to imagine God coming into the graveyard, pulling out a shovel and beginning to dig up graves. He tenderly pulls out the bodies, cleans off the faces and brushes off the lips. Bending down, closer and closer, he gives us the kiss of life—we are alive! Then he lifts us up, washes us and covers us with royal garments—the clothing of sons and daughters. He takes us to his own home, seats us with his own Son and adopts us into his own family. We become heirs of "every spiritual blessing" (Ephesians 1:3) and "unsearchable riches" (Ephesians 3:8), now and in the age to come. And finally, because of his great love for us, he offers us as a bride to his beloved Son. Amazing grace. Amazing God.

The Letter to the Ephesians reveals to us who we are in Christ, what God has done for us in Christ and how we should live in Christ. In spite of our sins and imperfections, God is accomplishing his perfect plan for us, the church. It is a plan that encompasses all eternity, offers sonship and life to the hopeless, and gives God all the "glory in the church and in Christ Jesus throughout all generations, for ever and ever! Amen" (Ephesians 3:21).

Someone has said that the book of Ephesians is shallow enough that the newest babe in Christ will not drown, but deep enough that theologians will never touch bottom. Reading it is like looking at the Grand Canyon by the light of a fireworks display. It is as deep as the mystery of God, as wide as the grace of God and as high as the love of God. And it speaks clearly to each and every one of us who are the church, a building that "rises to become a holy temple in the Lord" and "a dwelling in which God lives by his Spirit" (Ephesians 2:21-22).

This short letter is full of treasures and truths that are as eternal as God. It is saturated with words like "all, every, fullness, riches, mystery, love, unity, grace" and "glory." It speaks to our security in Christ, the amazing grace of God and the glory of the church—the building, body and bride of Christ (Ephesians 2:21, 4:16, 5:25). It illustrates our positions in Christ—we sit, we walk, and we stand (Ephesians 2:6, 4:1, 6:10-11 KJV). It reveals the work of Father, Son and Spirit in God's plan of redemption. It proclaims a love that is wide and long and high and deep. It encompasses God's eternal purpose—before creation, now and in the age to come. It portrays "one God and Father of all who is over all and through all and in all" (Ephesians 4:6). And finally, it is a call to the highest possible unity in the church, between Jews and Gentiles, husbands and wives, slaves and masters, children and fathers, and in the cosmos itself—the heavens and the earth (Ephesians 1:10). Yet, as is often the case with Scripture, it is ultimately a call to practical Christian living—you are sons of God; therefore live lives "worthy of the calling you have received....Be imitators of God" (Ephesians 4:1, 5:1).

Except for the Gospels, the book of Ephesians has had the greatest impact on my life and worldview as a Christian. Shortly after I was baptized, I decided to memorize this great letter. I glued verses on index cards and kept them in my shirt pocket for weeks. I read this book over and over and listened to it on tape again and again. I even played the cassettes while

I was sleeping in an attempt to absorb it subliminally! I pondered it, quoted it and talked about it. I wrote my own paraphrase. I studied and read commentaries and sermons about it.

It became apparent to me, even as a young Christian, that this letter of Paul's was not merely a manual of theology and Christian living, but a masterpiece of divine literature. God's breath and his fingerprints can be felt on every word, every thought, every consonant and vowel. Concepts and key words, patterns and themes, some obvious and some subtle, are woven together in such a rich and seamless way that the unity and genius of this short letter is quite breathtaking. Only a man completely inspired by God could produce such a perfect treatise of the Christian life. We can spend a lifetime pondering this small book and never run out of new insights or applications or reasons to be grateful and praise our wonderful God for it.

I am grateful to be able to recommend Tom's new study on the book of Ephesians. But I am even more grateful to consider him my friend. His book will help all of us gain a better appreciation of who we are in Christ and to love God's church more completely. The man who wrote it cherishes the kingdom and grapples with issues that are critical to the integrity and life of the church. I am always amazed at Tom's spirit of gratitude and peace. Although his body is in a degree of bondage to multiple sclerosis, he knows that he is free in the Lord and that he is seated with Christ even now in the heavenly realms. From this vantage point, he helps all of us to look at our lives and our problems from a heavenly perspective.

Tom is a Christlike man, and I know that what he has to share in this book will help us to be more like Christ ourselves. In the words of the old adage, We do not want to be so heavenly minded that we are of no earthly good. His book will not only help us to appreciate our heavenly call, but it will also spur us on toward love and good deeds—"for we are God's workmanship, created in Christ Jesus to do good works, which God prepared in advance for us to do" (Ephesians 2:10).

Henry Kriete
January 2001

Acknowledgments

I wish to thank the members of the Northwest region of the Boston church, where I serve as an elder, for their encouragement as we used this material in a recent study of the book of Ephesians. Special thanks also should go to Henry Kriete and Mike Van Auken. Henry graciously agreed to write the foreword at the very time I was being so moved by his own book, *Worship the King*. Mike is training under my friend, Gordon Ferguson, to serve as a teacher. He has long been interested in Ephesians and has provided some valuable material in the additional notes section in the back of the book.

I am always grateful for the exceptional work done by DPI's editorial and design staff. In particular, I am thankful for Lisa Morris and Kim Hanson who copyedited this book, for Tony Bonazzi who designed the cover and for Corey Fisher who designed the interior. I am also grateful for the many others at DPI who will do so much to make sure that this book gets into many hands.

I am thankful to God for my partnership in this ministry with Kelly Petre, whom God will use to take DPI to new heights. Working with Kelly for the past year has been pure joy. Kelly is a scholar, editor, friend and brother in Christ. He provided valuable assistance in the completion of this project.

And finally, I am thankful for that special person who has been my wife for more than thirty years and who gives me constant encouragement and support, as well as wise editorial advice. I have been so blessed to have her not only share my life, but to share in this publishing ministry with me for the last eight years. Sheila, I love you dearly.

Chance or Choice?
Introduction to Ephesians

Six billion people now live on this planet. Each day they go in at least six billion directions. There is no shortage of activity in our world. It is one busy place. But is there a plan? Is there any purpose behind the universe? Are we here for a reason? Did someone put us here who had a plan for our lives? When we ask such questions, we are wrestling with one of the greatest philosophical and spiritual issues of all time.

A number of years ago, I came across the writings of the French biochemist and sometime philosopher, Jacques Monod. He taught that life is just one big cosmic accident. He says we are here simply because our number came up in a Monte Carlo game. Although he admits that the universe is amazingly ordered and complex and that realities like the genetic code perplex him (translation: create problems for his philosophy), Monod does not believe that there ever was a plan. Everything you see around you, he says, is purely the result of chance. (If you find such certainty on the arrogant side, you and I are thinking similarly.)

Monod gets a good deal of attention and is frequently quoted by others who argue for a universe without meaning, but his arguments are not compelling even to many fellow scientists. A few years ago, an article in the *Boston Globe* described a gathering of highly regarded scientists who were coming together to discuss the spiritual conclusions that they felt their study of science was leading them to accept. The article described a growing number of scientists who believe that recent discoveries indicate that the universe was designed and that it has meaning.

Michael Turner, a physicist at the University of Chicago, has described the odds of the universe just coming into being

13

by chance and then not collapsing back on itself. He argues that this would be about the same odds as one would have if he tried to throw an imaginary microscopic dart across the universe to the most distant object we know (a quasar) in order to hit a bull's-eye that is only one millimeter in diameter.[1] It doesn't sound like he thought too much of the "it just happened by accident" idea.

There Is a Plan

This amazing universe of ours and the amazing things that go on even in our own bodies all point to the fact that there is a plan. As David wrote,

> The heavens declare the glory of God;
>   the skies proclaim the work
>   of his hands. (Psalm 19:1)

> I praise you because I am fearfully and wonder-
>   fully made;
>   your works are wonderful,
>   I know that full well. (Psalm 139:14)

Of course as Christians, we are not left just to conclude that there is a plan from what we see in the creation. God has sent prophets and apostles—and his own Son—to reveal to us plainly what that plan is and how we fit into it. The Letter to the Ephesians is a most important New Testament document because it deals specifically with this theme. It is all about God's plan.

Through the years I have had the opportunity to teach from Ephesians several times. On one occasion I titled my class "God's Great Plan." The next time I taught it, I changed the title to "God's Perfect Plan for Imperfect People." In this title there are three ideas that are important. First, there is a plan (see Ephesians 1:11). Life is not a collection of meaningless accidents. There is a reason for our existence. Life is a gift. It

---

[1] Rick Gore, "The Once and Future Universe," *National Geographic* (June 1983), 745-746.

has come to us not by chance, but because God has chosen to give it us. Second, it is a perfect plan. He whose work is flawless designed it. At times it will look to human eyes as though it has some fatal errors or that it has failed, but it will not fail. It will be fulfilled completely. Finally, it is a plan for imperfect people. This is the best news of all. It is a plan that deals with our humanity, with our sin and with our weaknesses.

If a brilliant leader were to tell me that he had the perfect plan for accomplishing some mission, and he were to tell me that my help was needed to execute it, the idea would be intimidating to me. Because I know how flawed I am, I would wonder how I could possibly fit into a perfect plan. Surely I would spoil things "big time." I might even wonder how perfect his plan was if he thought I was the one needed to help it work. If you have any tendencies to think in this same direction, Paul in Ephesians will help you. He will show us that the plan takes into consideration our failings and deals with them. There is something magnificent at the core of the plan—it is called "grace." Because of the presence of grace, our flaws will not stop the fulfillment of the plan. It is indeed a perfect plan for imperfect people. This is the reason the message is called "the gospel," the good news!

The Church in the Plan

In order to properly introduce the Letter to the Ephesians, we need to look at something else that makes it unique. It is the one letter in the New Testament that seems especially written to say that the ultimate fulfillment of God's plan is found in Christ and particularly, *in his church.*[2] Christ is the heart of the plan, but Christ and his church are inseparable. The church is not a footnote to the plan. It is not some little mention in the fine print. It is not some accessory you can add on after you already have the real deal. The church is right there with Christ at the *very center* of the plan, because the church was *his* plan. If you miss the church, you miss the

[2] Certainly, this idea is found many places in the New Testament, but in Ephesians it seems to be the central idea in Paul's mind as he wrote.

plan. That's not often well understood, even by many religious people, but we will see this message clearly as we dig into Ephesians.

Think about this for a moment: When Paul wrote this letter sometime between 60 and 65 AD, no student of history would have thought the church to be major player. Yes, by this time the church had spread in a remarkable way throughout the Roman Empire, but the disciples were still a tiny group—and a despised one at that. Outside the church, we would not have been able to find anyone who thought that these people were part of some great plan for the world. If there were those who thought there was some plan, it certainly would have looked more like the Roman Empire would be the fulfillment of it. Contrast the two candidates for a moment. On one side we have the awesome power of Rome. Never had one empire so dominated the world. On the other side, we have the church of Jesus Christ, a tattered, persecuted band of believers who worshiped a crucified man as God. And we are asked to believe that some great plan for mankind is being fulfilled in this second group? This is, in fact, the message of Ephesians.

Twenty centuries later, there are still people who think it is a foolish idea. But it is interesting to note that no one has said "Caesar is Lord" for thousands of years. Yet, today at the dawn of the twenty-first century, around the world, on all continents, in dozens of languages, men and women will confess that "Jesus is Lord," and his disciples still find in him power to live their lives. There will always be those who think God's plan is foolishness, but even by human standards, it doesn't look as foolish as it once did.

So, what can you expect to get from Ephesians? You can expect to hear good news for your life. You can expect to see a God who pours out his resources for you in amazing ways. You can expect to feel loved. But beyond this, you can expect to see in Ephesians how God is at work to bring you together with others and connect you to them in a way he always planned. You can expect to find principles that will enable the church on earth to be a colony of heaven.

But let's ask one important question: How will we know if the message of Ephesians is really getting into our hearts and minds? How will we know it is having the effect that God intended? Here's the answer: When we are deeply grateful that God has included us in his plan. When we have a passion in our lives for building up the body of Christ. When we are laying down our lives for our brothers and sisters. When we make it a priority to reach others so they can share God's grace with us. Interestingly, there is not one command or even admonition in Ephesians to evangelize, but we will not have really grasped its message until we have the same attitude as Paul when he wrote,

> Pray also for me, that whenever I open my mouth, words may be given me so that I will fearlessly make known the mystery of the gospel, for which I am an ambassador in chains. Pray that I may declare it fearlessly, as I should. (Ephesians 6:19-20)

We are here not by chance, but by God's choice. Ephesians will show us exactly what he had in mind for each of us and for us collectively as the body of Christ.

1 Chosen, Adopted, Blessed

Paul, an apostle of Christ Jesus by the will of God,

To the saints in Ephesus, the faithful in Christ Jesus:

²Grace and peace to you from God our Father and the Lord Jesus Christ.

³Praise be to the God and Father of our Lord Jesus Christ, who has blessed us in the heavenly realms with every spiritual blessing in Christ. ⁴For he chose us in him before the creation of the world to be holy and blameless in his sight. In love ⁵he predestined us to be adopted as his sons through Jesus Christ, in accordance with his pleasure and will—⁶to the praise of his glorious grace, which he has freely given us in the One he loves.

Ephesians 1:1-6

The apostle Paul was a man with a keen mind—a man who could hold his own with the intellectual heavyweights of his day. However, when Paul begins this letter, he does not begin it as an intellectual. He begins it as a humble man who stands in awe of God. In Ephesians Paul is going to brilliantly and with amazing economy of words describe God's plan in such a way that hardly any major Biblical theme is left out. Paul was an impressive and gifted man, but he does not begin Ephesians with any effort to impress us with Paul. He begins his letter as a man on his knees, as a man in worship, as a man bowing before God in gratitude. His example needs to train us.

First Comes Worship

Paul begins Ephesians giving praise to God for the blessings we have received from him in Christ. Paul will not waste any time in getting to the theme he will develop in this letter. He will quickly begin to use a host of words that show us that God has a plan. However, before he gets to those, he must first come before God in worship. His praise of God is tightly connected to the plan he will write about, but he starts by emphasizing the God who has the plan and who is worthy of praise.

Being disciples of Jesus is certainly about using our minds, but discipleship is much more than an intellectual exercise. We must be spiritual people who allow spiritual fruit to be produced in our lives. As we grow in our understanding of God's plan, the reason we are a part of it and the blessings that come to us because of it, praise will be the fruit that is found on our lips. We will be known as a grateful people who give honor to God for our blessings.

Paul had a message burning on his heart. The praise he gives to God is given in view of the message he is about to share with us. If you don't find yourself naturally breaking into praise, hang on. Paul is going to show you why you should.

Through Heaven's Eyes

As Paul praises God, he focuses on the way he has "blessed us in the heavenly realms with every spiritual blessing in Christ." Paul was writing this from prison, where he was held in chains (Ephesians 6:20), but these circumstances did not quench his spirit of praise. Paul understood the difference between what goes on in this world and what is true in the "heavenly realms." The Romans might lock him up; he might be mistreated; he might suffer greatly; but no physical circumstances could deprive him of the all-important spiritual benefits he had because he was in Christ.

The animated movie *The Prince of Egypt* depicted the life of Moses and included several powerful songs, including one titled "Through Heaven's Eyes." One stanza from the song asks,

> So, how can you see what your life is worth
> Or where your value lies?
> You can never see through the eyes of man.
> You must look at your life,
> Look at your life through heaven's eyes.[1]

What Paul is helping us do in Ephesians is to look at life through heaven's eyes. Disciples who do this see that they have been amazingly blessed in the ways that matter most. "We were chosen before the creation," he says, essentially. There was a *creation* and there is a *Creator*, but before he ever created, he had us in mind, and he was determined to benefit us in his great plan. Try this: Go outside on a clear, starry night. Take some time to just contemplate the universe. Allow yourself to be amazed. Then give praise to the God who made it all because he was committed to blessing you before he ever created the first thing. You may be facing some challenges, even some severe ones, but look at your life through heaven's eyes.

As I write, there are no metal chains on my legs and arms, but I do experience the invisible chains of multiple sclerosis. This disease, which has profoundly affected my life for the last ten years, can make one's arms and legs feel like lead and make simple tasks fairly complex. I don't understand all the reasons why God allows such things, but I have chosen to focus not on the things that are seen and are temporary, but on the things that are unseen and eternal. God had a plan for my life before the universe was created. He was for me then, and he is still for me now. He deserves my praise, and I will gladly give it to him.

In choosing to bless us before time began, God had two specific things in mind. He intended that we would be holy

[1] Words and music by Stephen Schwartz, "Through Heaven's Eyes," from the original motion picture soundtrack of *The Prince of Egypt* (Universal City: Dreamworks Records, 1998).

and blameless in his sight (v4) and that we would be adopted as his children (v5). Having said these two things, Paul then adds, "to the praise of his glorious grace" (v6). If we truly get the message of Ephesians, we will come away in awe of the grace of God, a theme Paul will return to again and again. As we get in touch with our own sinfulness (and Paul will help us with that in Ephesians 2), we will marvel at the "amazing grace" God has given which enables us to be absolutely blameless and without accusation in his presence. We will be deeply grateful that, though we foolishly tried to work out our own plan, we have now been forgiven and adopted as sons and daughters into his family.

As we go on in Ephesians, the plan will be more completely revealed, but even the early glimpses should bring us before God in praise of his grace.

Taking Inventory

1. What personal lessons do you need to learn from Paul's praise of God?

2. In what ways do you need to look at your life "Through Heaven's Eyes"?

3. How does knowing that you were in the mind of God before the creation of the world affect your thinking?

2 Amazing Grace

> In him we have redemption through his blood, the
> forgiveness of sins, in accordance with the riches
> of God's grace [8]that he lavished on us with all wis-
> dom and understanding. [9]And he made known to
> us the mystery of his will according to his good
> pleasure, which he purposed in Christ, [10]to be put
> into effect when the times will have reached their
> fulfillment—to bring all things in heaven and on
> earth together under one head, even Christ.
>
> Ephesians 1:7-10

At least twenty-five years ago I read a book with the title
Grace Is Not a Blue-Eyed Blond. The author's point was that a
lot of people who believe in Jesus have little understanding
of grace. I agreed with his premise, and a quarter of a century later, I am concerned that even among those who are serious disciples, we are sometimes superficially acquainted
with grace, and that is serious problem

When you look at the way Paul speaks of grace, it is
obvious that it was for him a rich and powerful truth. In the
previous paragraph he spoke of "glorious grace" (v6). Here
he speaks of "the riches of God's grace" (v7). Then he
makes the point that this grace from God was "lavished on
us" (v8). God has a great plan, and we are included in this
plan for one reason: *grace*. The grace of God is at the core of
the plan. Without grace this plan would not exist. If you
ever feel I am saying too much about grace in this book, I
offer no apology. It has been given too little emphasis and
this must change.

What *Does* It Mean?

As I wrote this chapter, I checked the dictionary and found eleven definitions of grace, ranging from beauty of movement to a short prayer before a meal. However, no dictionary definition of grace, even the one designated with the word "theology," is really adequate. "Unmerited favor" is technically correct, but it has the sound of something found in a manual. In contrast the Biblical doctrine of grace is the warm and transforming truth that our forgiveness, our relationship with God and the spiritual victories in our lives all come about because a loving and personal God has chosen to pay a great price to meet our deepest needs. Specifically, grace refers to the ultimate expression of God's love— Christ's atoning sacrifice for us while we were still sinners. Grace is the idea that those who deserve nothing are treated as if they deserved everything.

Most of the time, people become a part of some great plan because of their talent, their intelligence, their skill or their hard work. Since the 1960s many Americans have sought to be a part of the space program with the plan of going to the moon, to Mars and beyond. However, the requirements have been tough, as I witnessed firsthand in the 1970s, when a talented friend of mine saw his application turned down. NASA does not look over its list of candidates and then select several of them just on the basis of grace. I would doubt that NASA has the word "grace" in their vocabulary. You will also not find it in the policy manuals of the Fortune 500 companies or the National Football League. Who ever drew a starting assignment for a Super Bowl contender on the basis of grace?

But here is the remarkable message of the gospel: *It is by grace that we are all included in God's great plan* and are put on the most important team on earth. If you thought you were on God's team because of your intelligence, I would like to burst your bubble. If you thought it was because of your beauty or your personality or your physical strength, I need to tell you the truth. If you thought you got on the team the old-fashioned way, by *earning* your spot with hard work, I must tell you that your theology is a mess. No one is included in God's plan because of merit or performance.

Why Is It So Crucial?

If you are on the team today and fulfilling the plan of God, here is why: God gave you his grace, and you put your faith in his gift. Paul goes out of his way to describe grace in extraordinary terms. Later in Ephesians 2 he will come back to this theme to emphasize it again. Why did Paul feel compelled to give such prominence to grace?

We can't see into Paul's mind, but here are four reasons why grace needs great emphasis: (1) "salvation by grace" is the very heart of the gospel; (2) some people have a tendency to think that they deserve to be a part of God's plan or a tendency to teach that you must earn your place in it; (3) other people see their weaknesses clearly and thus have trouble believing that they can be a part of God's plan at all; and (4) it is grace that unites the church because it keeps us all dealing with each other from a position of humility.

Sadly, the doctrine of grace has been abused. Grace has been made an excuse for laziness, inactivity and lack of commitment. (We will address this problem when we get to Ephesians 2.) However, we must not make an equally serious mistake of emphasizing commitment in such a way that would marginalize grace. Every disciple must understand that he or she was included in God's great plan *and continues in that plan* for one reason: The riches of grace have been lavished on us by God with wisdom and understanding.

As a God who gives us what we do not deserve, our Father has revealed to us the "mystery of his will" (v9). He has always had a plan to do the most amazing things in Christ, and he made his purposes clear when "the times…reached their fulfillment" (v10). There is a gracious God behind this universe, and events have meaning because of him. Life is not a series of random accidents. It is the gift of God, who has plans and brings them to fulfillment.

As we read on, we will understand more fully how God intends "to bring all things...together under one head, even Christ" (v10). In Ephesians 1:22-23, we will take an in-depth look at Jesus as this cosmic Christ. As we grasp more details and gain more insight into the mystery of God's will, let us praise God for his amazing grace that allows us to be part of it all.

Taking Inventory

1. How would you compare the way Paul describes grace with the way you think about it? Do you describe grace to others the way Paul describes it? Is it for you a rich and powerful truth?

2. What fears or concerns do you have about emphasizing grace?

3. How does it affect you when you take your eyes off the grace of God and forget that he has lavished it on you?

3 Belonging to God

> In him we were also chosen, having been pre-
> destined according to the plan of him who works
> out everything in conformity with the purpose of
> his will, [12]in order that we, who were the first to
> hope in Christ, might be for the praise of his glory.
> [13]And you also were included in Christ when you
> heard the word of truth, the gospel of your salva-
> tion. Having believed, you were marked in him
> with a seal, the promised Holy Spirit, [14]who is a
> deposit guaranteeing our inheritance until the
> redemption of those who are God's possession—
> to the praise of his glory.
>
> Ephesians 1:11-14

In Ephesians 1:3 Paul begins a sentence that runs for twelve verses. That sentence in Greek translates into 279 words in the New International Version. In any language, this makes for one long sentence! It's as though Paul started talking about God's amazing plan and God's amazing grace, and he simply could not stop the cascade of words. Paul stands in awe of what God has done, and each thought he has about how God has blessed us leads to another.

As Paul returns to a theme introduced earlier—"we were also chosen"—he adds another detail. The one who chose us and who included us in his plan "works out every-thing in conformity with the purpose of his will" (v11). Paul may be thinking here about the way God works in the great events of history, but the message would equally apply to the details of our personal lives. (Wouldn't it all be the same to God?) Our lives may be filled with imperfections, but

God's plan is perfect. In everything God works for the good of those who love him and fits all the pieces together to accomplish his grand purposes.

In all of our lives there are hardships that bring up the "Why do bad things happen to good people?" issue. However, God's plan takes into consideration even the bad things and fits them into the bigger picture. The end result is that he makes his people winners (see Romans 8:28-39). Paul was in chains and in prison, but God was accomplishing his purposes even in that. Such a conclusion may be hard to accept emotionally, but God's plan will not be thwarted. The "everything" of Ephesians 1:11 and the "all things" of Romans 8:28 mean exactly what they say: God is at work in them all. Each of us must, with faith, apply this truth to our lives.

The Seal of Ownership

Here is why we can be so confident that God is going to work for good in all circumstances: *We belong to him.* He takes care of those who are his. When we were baptized into Christ, we were given the gift of the Holy Spirit (Acts 2:38), but Paul helps us see here that the reception of the Spirit marked us "with a seal." In the ancient world, a package or a crate that was being shipped would have a seal of ownership placed on it, indicating who it belonged to. In some cases the seal might be a unique symbol, somewhat akin to corporate logos today. When that seal was seen, there was no doubt about who the owner was. Paul says the Holy Spirit has been placed on us who are in Christ to clearly show that we belong to God.

We are the children of God. We belong to his family. We are not orphans in a dark, cold universe. We are a people belonging to God. What do you do with your own valuable things? All responsible people take care of what is theirs. I will soon be taking my car in for an oil change because I want to take care of what belongs to me. On a much more important level, I will be in touch with each of our children this week because I care about their lives — even though they are all grown. I first wrote this chapter on the birthday of my "son by marriage." He is now part of our family. I just called to encourage him and tell him how much I love him. I would do anything for him. He belongs to us. In the same way, each believer belongs to God. Each disciple is marked with God's seal of ownership. God looks down from heaven, and seeing his seal on us he says, *They belong to me, and I will care for them.*

The Earnest of the Inheritance

Paul adds another metaphor to help us appreciate who we are. He says the same Holy Spirit is also the deposit guaranteeing our inheritance. The word in Greek for deposit is *arrabon,* and the older versions translate it as "the earnest." A variation of the term is still in use today in the real estate world. Each time we have bought a home, we were required to put down what is still called "earnest money." This needs to be an amount of money large enough to clearly show the seller of the property that you are serious about your intentions. Just as my earnest money gives the seller of property assurance that I mean business, so the work of the Spirit in our lives now gives us assurance of the full inheritance that is to be ours.

At this point, let me urge you to be careful. When you think about the Spirit being given to us, do not just think personally and individually. The Spirit primarily is at work in *us,* not just at work in *me.* We Westerners — and particularly, we Americans — tend to be individualists. We think first about what is happening to "me." But the major evidence of the Spirit's presence in our lives is the way he is working *in us* to bring us together and to give us the power to function in unity as a body — which is a key concept in Ephesians. As it shows up again and again, I pray it will change our thinking about how God works in our lives.

We belong to God. I belong to God, and you belong to God, and *we* belong to God together. He has marked us with his own Spirit. The Spirit at work in us individually and collectively is his assurance of his faithfulness now and forever. No wonder Paul talks twice about us living for "the praise of his glory." We are marked by God for blessings, and we have countless reasons to be grateful.

Taking Inventory

1. To what challenge in your life do you need to apply the idea that God is at work in everything for our good?

2. How does it affect you to know that when God looks at the six billion people on earth, he very quickly knows that disciples are those who belong to him?

3. What do you see in the body of Christ that shows that the Holy Spirit has done something unique and special here?

4 Power Points

> For this reason, ever since I heard about your faith in the Lord Jesus and your love for all the saints, [16]I have not stopped giving thanks for you, remembering you in my prayers. [17]I keep asking that the God of our Lord Jesus Christ, the glorious Father, may give you the Spirit of wisdom and revelation, so that you may know him better. [18]I pray also that the eyes of your heart may be enlightened in order that you may know the hope to which he has called you, the riches of his glorious inheritance in the saints, [19]and his incomparably great power for us who believe. That power is like the working of his mighty strength, [20]which he exerted in Christ when he raised him from the dead and seated him at his right hand in the heavenly realms, [21]far above all rule and authority, power and dominion, and every title that can be given, not only in the present age but also in the one to come.
>
> Ephesians 1:15-21

It is not unusual for Paul to talk about prayer. However, it is a bit unusual for him to break into prayer in the midst of a letter, as he does at some length both here and in Ephesians 3:14-21. He first refers to the thanks he continually gives for these disciples. As with the Thessalonians to whom he had written earlier (1 Thessalonians 2:19), it would seem that they had become his joy and crown. He is deeply grateful for them and constantly brings them before God in prayer. He then describes three specific prayers that he prays on their behalf, and in so doing, he gives us a model of how to pray for one another.

To Know God Better

Paul gets first things first. He prays that they will be given the Spirit of wisdom and revelation so that they will know God better (v17). This is the ultimate goal of God's plan. The Bible is a love story of the God who wants to be known and who wants to teach us to know each other. The second, however, cannot really happen without the first. I would imagine that we have all experienced the frustration of wanting to know someone more deeply, only to find that they did not really desire for us to get to know them. Some people send out signals that seem to say, *Don't get too close.*

No such signals come from God. He wants us to know him, and he gives us the grace that allows us to know him. His plan is not just a plan to control our behavior and shape up our image. It's a plan to let us know him personally, deeply and in ever-increasing ways. His plan is that we would even *enjoy* him.[1]

As we engage in ministry, we must remember this: We are not trying to get people into a system, but into a life-changing relationship. We must pray for each other that we will know God better.

To Know the Hope and the Inheritance

Paul next uses a phrase that appears only here in the entire Bible. He prays that *the eyes of their hearts will be enlightened* so that they will understand the hope to which they have been called (v18). Paul is not talking about the organ that pumps blood to the body. Along with other Biblical writers, he uses "heart" to refer to that deepest part of man. He is praying here that at the very core of who they are, they will have spiritual eyes wide open to see what a profound hope all Christians have. Specifically, he wants them to grasp "the riches of his glorious inheritance in the saints" (v18).

[1] See my chapter on enjoying God in *Our God Is an Awesome God* (Woburn, Mass.: DPI, 1999), 149-152.

To have hope and to be confident about the inheritance that is coming to you is to be secure. This is clearly God's will for us. Our weaknesses and the unpredictability of life can make anyone feel insecure and uncertain. God wants us to see clearly that we are in his plan *and in his hands*. He wants us to understand that the end result of a life lived for him will be a rich inheritance. We don't "hope" that heaven will be there, as many in the world wistfully hope. We have a firm hope and are confident that we have been marked by the Holy Spirit to inherit God's riches. Even though we are still in the midst of the adventure, with the eyes of faith, we can see the end of the video—and we see that we are winners. This is the kind of vision that Paul is praying for disciples to have. He would not have prayed it if it were not possible for us all.

And so I pray that we will be done with fretting, hand-wringing and whining—our names are written in heaven! We are on our way there, whether sooner or later. Let us live not only as those who look through heaven's eyes, but as those who clearly have heaven in our eyes.

To Know the Power of the Resurrection

Paul finishes by praying that our spiritual eyes will see the power that is available to us who believe (v19). Each time the American space shuttle lifts off from Cape Canaveral, sent on its heavenward journey by those massive rocket engines, we see an awe-inspiring display of power. But the power it takes for man to break what the Canadian pilot and poet called "the surly bonds of earth," is nothing compared to the power that it took to break the bonds of death. Paul prays that Christians will understand that they have this power which broke Jesus free from sin, death and the grave, giving him the place of preeminence above every authority.

It is hard for the church to understand what it has, and easy to forget what we know. We look around in our fellowship, and we see talent and strengths; but we also see

weaknesses and signs of ordinariness. There is often something unusual going on among us, and at times it is quite
remarkable. But our personal efforts can bog down, our
activities can grow stale, and jealousy, pettiness and bitterness can show up in our relationships. The resulting lack of
growth and change can cause some people to become cyni-
cal and doubtful. We can become focused on negatives.
Sometimes the church is all too human, and this humanness
keeps us from seeing the divine. This is why Paul prays and
this is why we need to pray that we will realize what power
is available to us.

Because the power given to us is resurrection power, it
can enter into a valley of dry bones and make them live again
(Ezekiel 37). Because it is the power of him who is "far above
all rule and authority, power and dominion" (v21), it is
enough to overcome the staleness and even the darkness that
can creep into the church. Whenever disciples humble themselves and seek God's help, power surges in, and the church
is revived.

We must pray with Paul that we would open our eyes so
we can know God better, so we can claim our hope, and so
we can understand the power of God that is forever ours if
we just believe.

Taking Inventory

1. What have you learned about getting to know people
   that would help you to get to know God better?

2. How does your understanding of our hope in Christ
   affect you personally?

3. How should the idea of the church having "resurrection power" influence your thinking about what
   can happen in your local congregation?

5 The Cosmic Christ and His Cosmic Church

That power is like the working of his mighty strength, [20]which he exerted in Christ when he raised him from the dead and seated him at his right hand in the heavenly realms, [21]far above all rule and authority, power and dominion, and every title that can be given, not only in the present age but also in the one to come. [22]And God placed all things under his feet and appointed him to be head over everything for the church, [23]which is his body, the fullness of him who fills everything in every way.

Ephesians 1:19-23

At this point in his letter Paul begins to show us that the church is at the heart of God's great plan. However, as he introduces this idea, he must say more about the preeminence of Christ. To understand why the church is so important, we must appreciate the Christ who bought the church with his own blood. The church, which can seem just as human as any earthly group, has a central place in the divine plan because of its relationship to Christ.

The Cosmic Christ

It is often said that the theme of Colossians, another of Paul's prison letters, is the all-sufficiency of Christ. The Colossians were being influenced by those who said, "Yes, we need Christ, but we need other things as well." Paul wrote Colossians largely to deal with this inadequate view of Christ. This is not his main theme in Ephesians, but the passage we are now considering could easily appear in Colossians, because Paul describes here the Christ who is preeminent in the universe.

Christ is the One who is above all authorities—physical and spiritual. He is Lord of the entire universe. But how did he get to such a position? In yet another of his prison letters, Paul makes this clear:

> Who, being in very nature God,
>   did not consider equality with God
>   something to be grasped,
> but made himself nothing,
>   taking the very nature of a servant,
>   being made in human likeness.
> And being found in appearance as a man,
>   he humbled himself and became
>   obedient to death—
>   even death on a cross!
> Therefore God exalted him to the highest
>   place and gave him the name that is
>   above every name,
> that at the name of Jesus every knee should
>   bow, in heaven and on earth and under
>   the earth,
> and every tongue confess that Jesus Christ is
>   Lord, to the glory of God the Father.
> (Philippians 2:6-11)

Christ does not reign in the universe because he had a clever scheme to take *over*. No, instead, he had a plan to take *off* his divine nature and take *on* the nature of a servant. It was a plan to lose his life, not a plan to save it. He reigns over the cosmos today because God honors that kind of humility. (This needs to be one of our deepest convictions and a conviction that guides the decisions we make about our own lives.) He has been exalted to the highest place and his name is above every name *because God raised him up* and put him there. But make no mistake about it: Though he got there through humility, *he is there ruling over all,* and every knee will bow and every tongue will one day confess that Jesus Christ is Lord.

We who are Christians need to remember daily who it is that we serve. The glamour of the world, the power of politics and the success of businesses can sometimes impress us far too much. Now that we know who Christ is, we can see that Isaiah's words apply to him as they do to God:

> Surely the nations are like a drop in a bucket;
>   they are regarded as dust on the scales;
>   he weighs the islands as though they were fine
>   dust. (Isaiah 40:15)

Our Jesus is Lord of all. Man's power is nothing compared to Jesus' authority. We should love everybody, but be intimidated by nobody. We should show respect to all men (1 Peter 2:17), but be unashamed of our Lord before everyone. He is the cosmic Christ.

His Cosmic Church

The truth about Christ is amazing. It would be unbelievable if there were not so many "undeniables." And yet the statement that follows may be even more remarkable:

> And God placed all things under his feet and appointed him to be head over everything for the church, which is his body, the fullness of him who fills everything in every way. (Ephesians 1:22-23)

Paul is saying something here that is repeated throughout the New Testament. Christ has been placed over all things "for the church." This very human band of sinners, this combination of people with all kinds of baggage, now has the undivided attention and support of the Lord of the Universe. Christ died "for the church" and now exercises his divine power "for the church." Do we deserve such treatment? Absolutely not, but remember, this is the story of the grace that has been lavished on us with wisdom and understanding.

As Christ is the Lord of the cosmos, so the church, because of its relationship to Christ, becomes the most important group of people in the cosmos. Can we boast about that? We'd better not! (Ephesians 2:9). Should we be sobered by this and take our mission seriously? Absolutely! (Ephesians 4:1). Should we praise God for the grace that gives us such a purpose? Without a doubt (Ephesians 1:3, 6 and 12).

Just look at who Paul says we are. We are the body of Christ. Christ is the head, and we are his body (Ephesians 5:23). As amazing as it is, Christ has chosen to work through us in this world. He has chosen for us to be his hands and feet and arms and legs. He has chosen to show his heart and emotions to the world through us.

Paul describes the church as "the fullness of him who fills everything in every way" (v23). We are to be the fullness of Christ in the world. We are to be filled up with the character of Christ so that the world feels his impact two millennia after his resurrection. Our Lord, our Savior and our friend rules over the universe. He has chosen to work through us. But what if we fail? *He has no other plan.*

Taking Inventory

1. Read Revelation 1:12-18, another passage that describes, in a very different style of writing, the power of Christ. This passage was also written to Ephesus. What does Ephesians 1:19-23 have in common with this passage in Revelation? How does each affect you?

2. When you think about the church, do you focus more on the human side or the divine side? Why does it matter?

3. When you read the description of the church in Ephesians, what kinds of feelings, emotions or passions are stirred within you?

6 All of Us in Need

> As for you, you were dead in your transgressions and sins, [2]in which you used to live when you followed the ways of this world and of the ruler of the kingdom of the air, the spirit who is now at work in those who are disobedient. [3]All of us also lived among them at one time, gratifying the cravings of our sinful nature and following its desires and thoughts. Like the rest, we were by nature objects of wrath.
>
> Ephesians 2:1-3

If chapter one of Ephesians ends by showing us the heights to which God has taken Christ, chapter two begins by showing us the depths from which God in Christ has rescued us. In his letter to the Ephesians, as in his much longer and more famous letter to the Romans, Paul proclaims the gospel, the good news. But good news is only understood and appreciated in contrast to the bad news it has enabled us to overcome. So in both Romans and Ephesians, Paul not only tells us the good news, but he makes sure that we understand the bad news also. These opening verses of chapter two are designed to help us to be grateful by reminding us of exactly who and what we were before Christ came into our lives. Paul will quickly go on to a fuller presentation of the gospel, but if we minimize these verses, we will not appreciate what we have received (compare with 2 Peter 1:9).

In the Grip of Death

"As for you," Paul says (v1), as if to say, "Now listen, I am talking to you." If we do listen, we understand how bad our condition was. We were not just struggling or sick spiritually. We were *dead* in our transgressions and sins. The unrighteousness in our lives had disconnected us from the life of God (Ephesians 4:18). Sure, we still had *bios* (physical life), but we had no *zoe* (spiritual life). At one time we may have been giving ourselves over to every kind of impurity or we may have been nice, self-righteous religious people. Perhaps we were somewhere in between. No matter, we were all dead in our sins. Without Christ's intervention, we would have all died physically and then discovered how dead spiritually we really were.

There is nothing pretty about this picture. The news in these three verses is all bad. Mercifully, the next paragraph will bring us some wonderful relief, but we must not skip too quickly to the solution. We must come to grips with our need. Paul describes in some detail just what contributed to our state of spiritual death. First, we "followed the ways of this world" (v2). Instead of being concerned about pleasing God, we were more concerned about fitting in to the world around us. In one way or another we all bought into the world's message. We all believed the lie that "self" is supreme, or at least we doubted that God's plan could be fully trusted.

Second, we also "followed...the ruler of the kingdom of the air" (v2). This is a unique description of the devil, but there is no doubt that Paul has him in mind. Paul connects the world and the enemy. To follow one is to follow the other, because indeed, the world gets its so-called wisdom from Satan. Just listen to Jesus' rebuke of Peter:

Jesus turned and said to Peter, "Get behind me, Satan! You are a stumbling block to me; you do not have in mind the things of God, but the things of men." (Matthew 16:23)

Peter had challenged Jesus' plan to go to the cross because it did not make worldly sense. Jesus rightly saw Peter's logic as both the thinking of Satan and the thinking of men. They belong together. We may never have consciously dabbled in Satan worship, but we must understand that we are no better than those who have. There is no telling how many times we have all acted in ways that have immensely pleased this enemy of God. "The spirit who is now at work in those who are disobedient" (v2) was actively working in our lives at one time. We all allowed him to be there.

Third, we were dead because we gave in to the cravings of our sinful nature. This nature urged us down a path, and we willingly went where it led. We all naturally have various desires and thoughts that originate in our sinful nature. The appearance of those thoughts is what the Bible calls "temptation." The arrival of those thoughts on the screen of our minds is not sin, but it is a temptation to sin. Between the appearance of the temptation and the choice we make, is what has been called "a moral space." Within this space, we do have a choice. Outside of Christ, we lived a life filled with the wrong choices. Even our right decisions were tainted with wrong motives and became a source of satisfaction for the enemy.

We lived not "according to the Spirit" but "according to the sinful nature" (see the contrast in Romans 8:1-4). Sin became our master. We, by our choices, became its slaves (see Romans 6:12-14), and as such, we became "objects of wrath" (v3). This is the sad truth about where we all stood outside of Christ. No wonder Paul will, a few verses later, show how wrong it would be for any of us to boast.

All Have Sinned

There is a final observation we must make because it is important for understanding Ephesians. Did you notice that Paul started out talking about "you," and then in verse 3 switched his language to "we"? The "you" is in reference to the sin of the Gentiles, but then he says "we" were also right there and just as guilty as you. Here he is referring to the Jews. A major theme in Ephesians is that in Christ all the barriers and distinctions are brought down. Jew and Gentile, separated for so long by a wall of hostility, are brought into the same family. In order for this to happen, the Jews had to understand that they were just as guilty before God as the Gentiles and just as much in need of his grace. There is a powerful message here for any of us who may be tempted to think we are better than others because of our race, culture or religion. As one of my best friends puts it, "The best of us is a mess." But thanks be to God, this is not the end of the story. (I don't know about you, but I am ready for verse four!)

Taking Inventory

1. Some people have a hard time seeing the seriousness of their sin. Others are overwhelmed thinking about how great their sin has been. Which tendency do you have? Why is it important to know this?

2. In what ways can you now see that in your life you have "followed the ruler of the kingdom of the air"? When do you think you have brought him the most pleasure? What convictions does this give you now that you are a disciple?

3. Paul writes these words to disciples who had been completely forgiven. Write down two things that such a passage should produce in you as a forgiven disciple.

7 Saved by Grace

But because of his great love for us, God, who is rich in mercy, ⁵made us alive with Christ even when we were dead in transgressions—it is by grace you have been saved. ⁶And God raised us up with Christ and seated us with him in the heavenly realms in Christ Jesus, ⁷in order that in the coming ages he might show the incomparable riches of his grace, expressed in his kindness to us in Christ Jesus. ⁸For it is by grace you have been saved, through faith—and this not from yourselves, it is the gift of God—⁹not by works, so that no one can boast. ¹⁰For we are God's workmanship, created in Christ Jesus to do good works, which God prepared in advance for us to do.

Ephesians 2:4-10

The opening verses of Ephesians 2 left no doubt about our desperate need, and the present paragraph leaves no doubt about God's plan to deal with that need. Because we were dead in our sins, we had no way of supplying power that would generate change. But thanks be to God, who is rich in mercy!

Paul is going to make sure of two things in this section of the letter: (1) that we clearly understand that salvation is by grace and (2) that we understand what grace produces in us whenever it is received. Most distortions of true spirituality have to do with one of these issues. If we get both sides of the coin that Paul describes here, we will be on our way to a sound balance between life and doctrine.

Not *by* Works

Coming as we do from a world where what we receive is based largely on performance, it is difficult for us to understand that we are not saved, made right with God or justified by our own effort. Since we naturally *feel* more saved on days when we do good things than on days when we fail and sin, we may conclude that our performance does in fact play some role in saving us. What Paul teaches here is the same message that he described in depth in the Letter to the Romans: "It is by grace you have been saved, through faith" (v8). The plain and simple message of the gospel is that we are saved (made right with God) when we stop trusting in our own works and put our faith (our trust) in what Jesus Christ has done for us. This is the message of radical grace and radical faith. It is amazing — shocking, even.

Paul seems to anticipate our hesitancy to embrace this, and he drives his message home, almost relentlessly, in verses 8 and 9:

- It is by grace you have been saved, through faith.
- This is not from yourselves.
- It is the gift of God.
- It is not by works.
- No one can boast.

I suppose he could have gone on to say more, but it is hard to see how he could have made himself any clearer. Though this idea is hard for us to accept, it is vital that we understand that our reconciliation to God is established by our trust in what Christ has done for us and not by *any* righteousness of our own. Read each of the phrases above again carefully, to make sure you feel the full impact.

Once we get past the shock, we start understanding why the gospel is such good news. If being right with God were based on performance, we would all fail the test. Paul has already described how we performed in the previous verses and made it clear that for *all of us,* our performance made us objects of wrath (Ephesians 2:3). But into that dark picture burst the person of Jesus who lived without sin and offered himself as the atoning sacrifice for sins (1 John 2:2). Now all of us who want a relationship with God can have that relationship through our faith in his blood (Romans 3:25).

But here is what we must keep straight: It is his work, his sacrifice, his righteousness and his life that saves us. We must continually reject the thinking that it's our righteousness. According to Paul's letter to the Galatians, this is a fatal mistake (see particularly Galatians 5:4) and one we must pray we will never make. Having said that, I don't want to leave the impression that understanding all the implications of grace is something that will happen quickly. It strikes me that Paul spent his entire life trying to grasp the depths of grace, while realizing that in this world he could never fully comprehend such things (see Ephesians 3:18-19).

But *for* Good Works

Second, we must understand from this passage what grace produces when it is accepted. Paul may describe this only in verse 10 here in chapter 2, but in some ways, most of chapters 4, 5 and 6 are an expansion of this idea. While it is absolutely true that it is not by (our) works that we are saved, Paul adds, "For we are God's workmanship, created in Christ Jesus *to do good works,* which God prepared in advance for us to do" (v10, emphasis added). Should you expect good works from disciples who are saved by grace? Absolutely. Grace did not come to just give us a ticket to heaven. Grace was given to bring us to God while we are in this world and to transform our lives so that we become like God in heart and character (see Ephesians 5:1-2). If you are not willing to submit to God so that this can happen, you don't really want what grace produces. You really have no interest in being saved in a Biblical sense.

Show me someone who says, "I am saved by grace," but has no interest in obeying Christ and changing to be like him, and I will show you someone who really has no appreciation for grace, no trust in it and no benefit of it. It is here that we see the connection between grace and discipleship. We are saved by grace, not by our discipleship. But grace is given to make us disciples (see Titus 2:11-12). If you don't want the result (being a disciple of Jesus), you would not want the gift (the grace of God). There are some who believe that they are saved by becoming disciples and that grace is just a nice extra, maybe for the tougher days. There are others who believe that they are saved by grace but show little or no interest in living as disciples. Both are dead wrong.

We are saved by grace. Only grace could have brought the dead to life. But being saved means being brought under the Lordship of Jesus so that we might live—not for ourselves, but for him who died for us (2 Corinthians 5:15). When we find someone who has truly put his trust in God's grace, we will have found someone who is devoted to being a disciple. Can we still say then that only disciples are saved? Without a doubt. But they are not saved because they do five or ten things that disciples do. They are saved because they turned away from self-effort and put their trust in Christ, allowing God's grace to re-create them in Christ Jesus to live as disciples. This is a difference we must understand.

Taking Inventory

1. Why is salvation by grace such good news to you personally?

2. When do you slip into thinking that your relationship with God is based on a performance model?

3. How do you know that someone who does not have a disciple's heart also has no faith in God's grace?

4. When we understand the correct connection between grace and works, why must boasting be completely excluded?

8 Destroying Division

> Therefore, remember that formerly you who
> are Gentiles by birth and called "uncircumcised"
> by those who call themselves "the circumcision"
> (that done in the body by the hands of men)—
> [12]remember that at that time you were separate
> from Christ, excluded from citizenship in Israel
> and foreigners to the covenants of the promise,
> without hope and without God in the world.
> [13]But now in Christ Jesus you who once were far
> away have been brought near through the blood
> of Christ.
>
> Ephesians 2:11-13

The World Almanac 2000 contains a chapter on what life will be like in the twenty-first century. The author stresses two themes: technology and tribalism. What he means by the first is obvious. What he means by the second is that human beings will continue to band together with others like themselves and separate themselves from those who are different. In his opinion we will see in the twenty-first century the same thing we have seen in all the others. The only difference is that we will be able to accentuate those differences with a more high-powered technology. If the last century and particularly the last ten years of that century is any indication, the author is on target. Tribalism and the negative, sometimes ruthless, treatment of others that often goes with it, was and still is seen from Kosovo to Indonesia, from Chechnya to Rwanda. In our own country the clash between races and cultures is still with us and often turns ugly. In spite of progress, the Western nations are still very segregated and tainted by racism. Add to this the hostility we often find between men and women, and the kind of ugly divisions we see in modern families, and we realize how much we need something that will bring peace.

Human history in many ways is one long story of conflict and division, and this passage in Ephesians addresses this problem. Look closely at Ephesians 2:11-22 and you will see words like "separate," "excluded," "far away," "barrier," "wall of hostility" and "foreigners and aliens." Paul recognizes that the world is a divided world, but he also sees that it is God's great plan to tear down those barriers and walls that divide and bring men and women of all kinds together in Christ. Again, look closely, and you will see an entirely different set of words that describe what happens in Christ: "brought near," the "barrier...destroyed," "making peace," "reconciled," "death [to] their hostility," "fellow citizens" and "joined together." Here we have a major theme in the Letter to the Ephesians: It is not only God's plan to give us peace with him, but it is a central part of his plan to give us peace with each other in the church of Jesus Christ.

Jews and Gentiles

Paul is, of course, referring here primarily to the division between Jews and Gentiles, but that broken relationship should be seen as one that symbolizes countless others. If the cross of Christ could heal the rift between Jew and Gentile and bring them together, then there is no division that cannot be healed. Not too many years before he wrote this, Paul was probably one of those rabbis who began every day by thanking God that he was not a Gentile. The walls of Jerusalem were not as thick as the walls of division that separated these two groups.

Gentile invaders from Syria (the Seleucids) had come to Jerusalem one hundred and fifty years earlier. They captured the city and desecrated the temple by sacrificing pigs on the altar in honor of pagan gods. If you know anything about the

Middle East, you probably know that the people there have a long memory. Incidents like this were not forgotten and probably influenced certain rabbis who taught that the Gentiles were created for only one purpose: to stoke the fires of hell.

Paul does remind the Gentile disciples that at one time they were separate from Christ (Greek for "Messiah"), probably meaning they were isolated from the promises of the Savior whom God was going to send for his people. They were excluded from citizenship in Israel and were foreigners to the covenants that God had made with the Jews. They had not received God's special revelation about himself, and as he points out in Romans 1, they had not even lived up to what they could have naturally known.

> Furthermore, since they did not think it worthwhile to retain the knowledge of God, he gave them over to a depraved mind, to do what ought not to be done. (Romans 1:28)

The end result is that they were "without hope and without God in the world" (v12).

Near, Far, Whoever You Are

Paul describes the Gentiles as those who were once "far away." This is something we all need to understand. Even the Jews, who by grace had been given more revelation and were somewhat closer, were still far away—as is made clear in the first verses of Ephesians 2 and treated at length in Romans 2. We must understand that being far away from God results in our being far away from each other. Ironically, what helps us all to be closer to one another is to realize how far away all of us are from God, apart from the cross, about which he will shortly have more to say. Self-righteousness does as much to divide us from others as anything else. In fact, it is almost always present in some form whenever there is division. When we realize how far away we were and how much we needed to be brought near by the blood of Christ, it humbles us and opens the door for living life on level ground with others. It is hard to be harsh and judgmental of others when you realize, "I need grace just as much as they do."

We have been brought near, Paul says, "through the blood of Christ" (v13). God became flesh and blood in Jesus. God endured pain in his flesh in Jesus. God poured out his righteous blood for us in Jesus. We may have thought we could draw near with hours of prayer, with our own works, maybe even with our harsh denial of the flesh (Colossians 2:23). But the only thing that will bring a black man, a white woman, an Asian teenager, a Latino father, an Indian mother or anyone else near to God is the blood of Christ. And once we realize that all of us get there in exactly the same way, there is no longer any reason for division among us.

Taking Inventory

1. How have you seen man's tendency toward division and conflict show up in your own personal life?

2. How, at one time, were you "far away," and how did that affect your relationship with others?

3. When do you tend to be judgmental and self-righteous? How does verse 13 help you to deal with this?

9 Peace Plan

For he himself is our peace, who has made the two one and has destroyed the barrier, the dividing wall of hostility, [15]by abolishing in his flesh the law with its commandments and regulations. His purpose was to create in himself one new man out of the two, thus making peace, [16]and in this one body to reconcile both of them to God through the cross, by which he put to death their hostility. [17]He came and preached peace to you who were far away and peace to those who were near. [18]For through him we both have access to the Father by one Spirit.

[19]Consequently, you are no longer foreigners and aliens, but fellow citizens with God's people and members of God's household, [20]built on the foundation of the apostles and prophets, with Christ Jesus himself as the chief cornerstone. [21]In him the whole building is joined together and rises to become a holy temple in the Lord. [22]And in him you too are being built together to become a dwelling in which God lives by his Spirit.

Ephesians 2:14-22

There were statements in the writings of Isaiah that let the Jews know hundreds of years before Christ that it was God's plan to show his favor to the Gentiles as well as to the Jews (Isaiah 9:1, 42:6, 49:6, 22). Few Jews had been willing to embrace these ideas or to look for their fulfillment. Those who did were usually looked on with suspicion. When Jesus came, he made it clear very early in his ministry that fulfilling Isaiah's words would be a priority for him. His teaching on this theme did, of course, get him in big trouble in his hometown right off the bat (Luke 4:25-29). Paul says, "For he himself is our peace, who has made the two one" (v14). This was not just an idea Paul developed later after reflecting on the message of Jesus. It was clearly Jesus' intention through-out his ministry to include all men and women, regardless of race, in his family. His message was first for the Jew, but also for the Gentile.

Paul says Jesus "destroyed the barrier, the dividing wall of hostility" (v14). He ultimately and with finality did this at the cross, which Paul will emphasize in verse 16. Throughout his ministry, however, Jesus worked to destroy barriers. He treated women differently. He treated children differently. He treated Samaritans differently. He treated Gentile centurions differently. He treated lepers differently. He had a former Roman-hater (Simon the Zealot) in his band of apostles, along with a former Roman loyalist (Matthew the tax collector). He brought people together by treating them all the same.

He Is Our Peace

Interestingly, Paul does not say that Jesus is our peace-maker, but that "he himself is our peace" (v14). Jesus does more than just help Jews and Gentiles negotiate a peace treaty. He himself becomes the actual source of their peace. In regard to the situation of the Jews and Gentiles, Jesus fulfilled the old law (Matthew 5:17), and then in his death ended its role. That old covenant, particularly with its many ceremoni-al requirements and regulations, was a barrier between Jews and Gentiles. Jesus fulfilled the law and then established a new basis for fellowship with God that would be true for all people, regardless of race or background.

"His purpose" was nothing short of creating "one new man out of the two" (v15). The New English Bible says it was his purpose to create "a single new humanity." This would seem to be the very idea that Paul had in mind. In Christ we all have an entirely new identity, not tied to whatever it was that we were before. This is why an African black, a European Caucasian, an Asian and a Latino can all be brothers or sisters in the same fellowship. All of them have a new identity which transcends their origins. They are now "children born not of natural descent, nor of human decision or a husband's will, but born of God" (John 1:13). Men and women from widely divergent backgrounds are reconciled to God and then to each other through the cross, by which "he put to death their hostility" (v16).

Paul is certainly talking here about the way that Christ fulfilled and then replaced the law. He sees this as the death of something that created hostility between Jews and Gentiles, but there is a message here that goes far beyond the Jew-Gentile issue and that applies to every human conflict and division. It does not matter what the source of tension or separation might be, the cross of Christ will deal with it. Whenever people of any background come to the cross, admit how much they need forgiveness and understand the need to take up the cross themselves and die to their pride, we will see people come together. Then they too will say, "Jesus is our peace." They will know that something has happened which must be of God.

We Are His Family

At the end of Ephesians 1 we were introduced to how important the church is in the plan. Now we begin to see what the church is to really be. It is first of all the "one body" (v16) where all are reconciled to God and to each other. It is the place where no one is to be treated as a foreigner or an alien, but everyone is a fellow citizen of the same kingdom and a brother or sister in the same household (v19). Whenever the fellowship in the church stops feeling like family — in the best sense of that word — we have gotten off track. When you think of the church as a big organization and yourself as a cog in the machinery, something is wrong. A God who is rich in mercy has loved us into the church, and he brought us into the church to live a life of love (more on this in Ephesians 5). God's plan is never to do something in a mediocre way. He comes to people who are divided, but he is not interested in just getting us to tolerate each other or coexist. He comes to take us all the way to "family," all the way to deep sharing and deep caring.

Paul will go on to say that the church is a building (v21), but it is clear that he is referring to one that is spiritual, not one built of brick and mortar. The church is a spiritual building in the sense that it becomes the dwelling of God. "Building" is just a metaphor. The church is the people, and it is in the people that you find God at work through his Spirit (v22). But even spiritual buildings must have foundations, and this one is "built on the foundation of the apostles and prophets, with Christ Jesus himself as the chief cornerstone" (v20). What makes the church of Jesus Christ the unshakable kingdom is this foundation. It is built on the message that came from God's men and on Christ himself—who not only taught the truth but who, through the cross, took down all the barriers to true fellowship.

Taking Inventory

1. What relationships do you have in the kingdom of God that you would have likely never had outside of Christ? How amazed are you about this?

2. As you follow Jesus closely, are there any changes that need to take place in the ways that you think about certain types of people?

3. Have you ever felt like a foreigner, even in the fellowship of the church? Who do you know who might feel like that now? What will you do to tear down the wall?

10 The Prisoner with a Purpose

> For this reason I, Paul, the prisoner of Christ Jesus
> for the sake of you Gentiles—
>
> Ephesians 3:1

Before we go on to look at more of Paul's message, we need to stop and take a good look at the one sentence that begins Ephesians 3. It is actually an aborted, incomplete sentence—one Paul never finished. We modern editors would correct it, yet it makes such an important statement. It says simply, "For this reason I, Paul, the prisoner of Christ Jesus for the sake of you Gentiles...." We have already pointed out that Paul wrote this while in chains (Ephesians 6:20). He was under arrest, held as a prisoner by the Roman government. We can only guess as to which imprisonment this refers to, but in any case, there would have been no doubt to his captors that he was their prisoner.

With Different Eyes

But Paul looked at his life in a completely different way. And this is the key for all who would be spiritual overcomers. We must have the eyes of our hearts opened to see circumstances in ways that ordinary people do not see them. Paul saw himself not as a prisoner of Rome, but as the prisoner of Christ.

With this language, has Paul suddenly departed from the glorious themes of God's grace and rich mercy that we saw in the first two chapters of Ephesians? Is he now shifting to an entirely different way of viewing his experience with God? Is he now thinking that he is locked up, tied down and put in a miserable circumstance by Christ? The answer to all these questions is no. There is a seamless connection between what Paul had already written and what he says here. He has not for a moment forgotten God's grace and love. On the contrary, he is a captive of that love. It compels him, constrains him and controls him (2 Corinthians 5:14, NIV, KJV, NASB). What God had done was so great and so good that it had become the driving and dominant force in his life.

A chain may have bound him to a Roman guard, but Paul saw himself in a much more important way as one bound to Christ. He refused to see himself as a victim of Rome, but as the possession of Christ. Yes, he was a prisoner. Yes, something restrained him, but he chose to see himself as one under the control of Christ, not as one whose fate was determined by capricious men.

Being a prisoner sounds negative. Who would want it? Yet Paul saw being a prisoner of Christ as something positive. The phrase surely affirms that he was a man with a mission and a purpose. Even if he was suffering, it was for the greatest of all causes. Like Paul, we must learn not to look just at our outward circumstances, but at the more significant spiritual condition in which we find ourselves in Christ. William Barclay says that Christians always have a double life and a double address. Normally, a double life is not a good thing; but what he means, of course, is that along with each outward circumstance there is the corresponding deeper spiritual reality. Whatever may be happening to us externally, who we are in Christ is not changed, and who we are in Christ is the more important of the two. In Paul's life, Christ was far more influential than Rome. The former would shape his life, and the latter could not ruin it.

For the Sake of Others

Notice this little fragment of a sentence carefully. Paul doesn't just say that he is a prisoner of Christ, but that he is a prisoner of Christ "for the sake of you Gentiles." When we are bonded to Christ, we are bonded to his mission. "The Son of Man," Christ said, "did not come to be served, but to serve, and to give his life as a ransom for many" (Mark 10:45). Christ came not for his own sake, but *for the sake of others.*

Paul understood that as a disciple he was bound to Christ, not just for his own sake, but for the sake of others. He was a prisoner of Christ, not just so that he might be saved, but so many others might come to God through his message. God had revealed to him the mystery that Paul will mention three times in the next few verses. But why? Paul understood clearly that it was in order that he might be a servant to others, as he expressed to the church in Corinth:

> For we do not preach ourselves, but Jesus Christ as Lord, and ourselves as your servants for Jesus' sake. For God, who said, "Let light shine out of darkness," made his light shine in our hearts to give us the light of the knowledge of the glory of God in the face of Christ. (2 Corinthians 4:5-6)

Paul also wrote that when the light of revelation shines in our hearts, showing us the glory of God in Christ, it should change us. We must, from that point forward, no longer live for ourselves, but for the sake of Christ and for the sake of others. At the very point in his life when Paul could have fallen into self-pity over his chains and his confinement, he took this message to heart and remembered that he lived, not for himself, but for the sake of others.

We live in a world where people do some good things for others, but where there is, nevertheless, an unending stream of messages encouraging us to live for ourselves. How many ads do we see or hear telling us that we deserve to do things just for our own pleasure? In our flesh, we all want to believe these messages, but if we are bonded to Christ, we will see that this is not our mission. We will recognize that this is not God's plan. Rather, it is his plan that we all live for the sake of others.

The bottom line? As a prisoner for Christ, we are set free to serve others, and this is a freedom that produces abundant fruit.

Taking Inventory

1. What situation in your life do you need to view differently because of who you are in Christ?

2. How can seeing yourself as the possession of Christ transform the way you look at this circumstance in your life?

3. When are you most tempted to have self-pity?

4. What will a commitment to live for the sake of others mean in your life? What decision will it prompt in you today or this week?

11 The Amazing Mystery

Surely you have heard about the administration of God's grace that was given to me for you, [3]that is, the mystery made known to me by revelation, as I have already written briefly. [4]In reading this, then, you will be able to understand my insight into the mystery of Christ, [5]which was not made known to men in other generations as it has now been revealed by the Spirit to God's holy apostles and prophets. [6]This mystery is that through the gospel the Gentiles are heirs together with Israel, members together of one body, and sharers together in the promise in Christ Jesus.

[7]I became a servant of this gospel by the gift of God's grace given me through the working of his power. [8]Although I am less than the least of all God's people, this grace was given me: to preach to the Gentiles the unsearchable riches of Christ, [9]and to make plain to everyone the administration of this mystery, which for ages past was kept hidden in God, who created all things.

Ephesians 3:2-9

In all honesty, you may have to read the passage before us more than once to get the full impact. (I had to read it and ponder it several times before I felt ready to write about it.) Paul is sharing with us something he found quite remarkable—but two thousand years removed from his experience, we may not immediately see what is so amazing. Let's give Paul a chance to explain.

An Unexpected Revelation

The first thing that astounds Paul is that God has made known "the mystery." This word was first used back in Ephesians 1, and now it appears four times in this short passage. In Paul's day the mystery religions had become quite popular among the masses and were serving to fill a spiritual void. These religions, including the popular Mithraism, were known for their often bizarre initiation ceremonies, during which the inductee would be told some secret insight. This insight was something that the cult members would never divulge to the uninitiated. This secret knowledge is what bound the members of the group together. But we must not think Paul had any interest in turning faith in Jesus into a mystery religion. Paul's use of the word "mystery" bears no resemblance to the way it was used in the cults.

The mystery for him is clearly defined in verse 6:

> This mystery is that through the gospel the Gentiles are heirs together with Israel, members together of one body, and sharers together in the promise in Christ Jesus.

God's plan to bring Jews and Gentiles—all men and women—together was a mystery in the past. It had not been revealed in earlier generations, and there was no clear understanding about how it would be accomplished. Most did not think it would ever be accomplished. But now after all these years, writes Paul, the mystery had been revealed that showed how the hostilities could be ended and how all men and women could become part of the same family, through the cross. Furthermore, what had been made known to Paul could now be preached to everyone. It was no longer to be concealed from anyone.

It is hard for us to understand how amazed Paul would have been to learn this mystery. The contempt between Jews and Gentiles was so great that reconciliation seemed impossible. As a Pharisaic Jew, Paul certainly would have never dreamed that there might be such a plan. His training and culture would have created in him no desire for this. It was certainly not anything he believed in or was looking for, prior to his encounter with Jesus on the Damascus road.

A Surprise Choice

If the first miracle for Paul was that there was such a plan to bring people together, the second miracle was that God would choose *him* to be the chief spokesman for it! I remember reading a liberal scholar once who said that Paul himself *discovered* the key to Jew-Gentile unity. Paul would be quick to tell you he did no such thing. Discoveries are made by seekers, and we give such seekers awards and recognition for their efforts and their findings. Paul does not see this as something he discovered. No, it came about by the "administration of God's grace" (v2). It was something that God had made known to him by revelation (v3). Paul simply received what God put before him, and he felt that in no way did he deserve credit for this message or its spread. Perhaps, recalling his attitudes and behavior before the Damascus road, his own assessment of himself was that he was "less than the least of all God's people," and it was purely grace that allowed him to preach to the Gentiles the unsearchable riches of Christ (v8).

In his days as a Pharisaic Jew, Paul had not been a visionary or reformer seeking to overcome the gulf between the racial factions. He had been a hard-liner who strongly, even violently, opposed the message of Jesus (a teacher whose message clearly showed that God loved the Gentiles, too). And so, for Paul it was remarkable that God in his grace would allow him to repent, allow him to be forgiven, and allow him to preach this mystery. He felt in his heart that he was "less than the least" — as far down as you can go.

For Us, Too

The historical circumstances of our lives are very different from Paul's. Almost none of us have a background even remotely like Paul's first century Judaism, but we need to see our place in God's plan just the way Paul did. We need to have a profound sense that we do not deserve this opportunity. We need to find it remarkable that through God's providence we received the message of Jesus, and we need to be amazed that he can and will use us to bring his message of forgiveness and reconciliation to other people. From Paul's example we learn that it's not a problem to see yourself as a very flawed human being, as long as you quickly see that through God's grace you can be a significant human being.

The mystery Paul is talking about here is God's plan to unite all people in Christ, but it is also something of a mystery to me, in another sense, that I have been included in the plan and given an opportunity to make a difference. I know my failures; I know my weaknesses. I know well the times of faithlessness and doubt. I don't know if I feel "less than the least," but sometimes I feel pretty close to that. But the message of the gospel, made clear in Ephesians, is that we are now servants "of this gospel by the gift of God's grace given [us] through the working of his power" (v7).

As Paul shares how remarkable it is to be involved in this great plan of God, hopefully all of us will do some marveling of our own when we consider who we are and what God has called us to.

Taking Inventory

1. Try putting yourself in Paul's place. What would have caused him to so drastically change his attitude toward the Gentiles?

2. Has the message of Jesus caused you to drastically change your attitude toward any group of people?

3. List three reasons why it is remarkable that you are a disciple of Jesus and a member of God's family.

4. What does the exercise above cause you to want to be or to do?

12 Through the Church ...the Wisdom of God

> His intent was that now, through the church, the manifold wisdom of God should be made known to the rulers and authorities in the heavenly realms, [11]according to his eternal purpose which he accomplished in Christ Jesus our Lord. [12]In him and through faith in him we may approach God with freedom and confidence. [13]I ask you, therefore, not to be discouraged because of my sufferings for you, which are your glory.
>
> Ephesians 3:10-13

Look around. What do you see? People, buildings, highways, forests, rivers, mountains, animals, machines. However, what we do not see with our physical eyes is even more important than what we do see. Behind the obvious events of life, there is a great spiritual conflict going on. The forces of evil are arrayed against the forces of God. This is not the stuff of children's stories or of ancient mythology. This is reality. We will see this with the greatest clarity when we get to Ephesians 6, but here in this passage, Paul makes a most important reference to the struggle. Here he refers to "the rulers and authorities in the heavenly realms." In Ephesians 6:12 Paul is clear about who is being described:

> For our struggle is not against flesh and blood, but against the rulers, against the authorities, against the powers of this dark world and against the spiritual forces of evil in the heavenly realms.

It is important to make this identification in order that we might understand what Paul is saying in this text about the role the church plays.

A Sign of Victory

It should be clear to us by now that one of God's greatest concerns and one of the greatest objectives of his plan is to bring people together in the church and for there to be unity. Eight times in the New International Version we find the word "together" in Ephesians. If it is God's will to bring people together, you don't have to have a lot of "smarts" to guess what the objective would be for the powers of this dark world. Though unseen, they are at work as Satan's messengers, seeking to plant selfishness, suspicion, jealousy, distrust, envy and hatred in the hearts of people, thus producing division wherever they can. Obviously, they target different racial and ethnic groups; they nurture nationalism and tribalism. But they go further and bore their ways into the hearts of families and neighbors. They wage war on the plans of God. No place is off limits for them, and their success is not something that can be doubted. We see examples of it everywhere we turn.

But into this divided world, God sent his Son, who came and preached peace and then laid down his life as the ultimate peace offering. He has a peace plan, and it works every time people respond to him. Those who come to him at the cross and crucify their pride, arrogance and selfishness truly come together as a new family in the church. When this happens, as it did in the first century and as it is happening in our day, *the manifold wisdom of God is made known to rulers and authorities in the heavenly realms.* In other words, in the community of the cross, the church of Jesus, it is made clear to these powers of darkness and these spiritual forces of evil that God is overcoming and defeating all of the nastiness they have planted in people's hearts.

The casual reader will sometimes think this passage is saying that the church is being used by God to make the gospel known to the world. The church is certainly used to do that, but this passage is making a different point. The church is essentially God's way of saying to the forces of darkness, "Look at all these people you divided. God is bringing them back together and teaching them to love and care for each other." Specifically, Paul says that it is "the manifold wisdom of God" that is made known to the evil empire (v10). The word "manifold" could be translated "many-colored," but it refers to that which has many features and a variety of applications. God's wisdom may seem like foolishness to men (1 Corinthians 1:18), but it is rich and full of power and capable of uniting all manner of people who seemed impossible to unite. All of this, Paul says, was "according to his eternal purpose which he accomplished in Christ" (v11). God has a plan, and as you and I unite with others in the church, we fulfill God's eternal purpose!

With Freedom and Confidence

Before Paul turns to his final burst of prayer and praise that will conclude part one of this letter, he adds two footnotes to his discussion. First, he reminds the disciples that through our faith in Christ, we have unrestricted access to God. Perhaps it was his reference to the spiritual warfare that caused him to think of this, but for whatever reason, he adds assurance here that believers can "approach God with freedom and confidence" (v12). While the rulers and authorities in the heavenly realms have nothing but our destruction on their minds, our God cares for us, and we can come to him freely and often. The Old Testament Jew usually came to God in fear and trembling, but the word "confidence" here (and in Hebrews 4:16) in Greek actually means that Christians can come to God with boldness. Such is the amazing state of grace that we enjoy. We, who on our own were objects of wrath, now enjoy the freedom to come to God boldly with our needs and requests.

These words of assurance are finally connected by the word "therefore" to one last thought. "I ask you, therefore, not to be discouraged because of my sufferings for you, which are your glory" (v13). Those who received this letter knew, of course, that Paul wrote from prison. With their leader and their hero in captivity, they could have easily been worried and distressed. But Paul is reminding them that no government or circumstance can take away their access to God. "Don't let it bother you," Paul says in so many words. "Because of our relationship to God, even our sufferings are turned into glory!" God has a plan, and man will not undo it.

Taking Inventory

1. How real is the unseen realm of the spiritual world for you? Are the powers of this dark world as real for you as God is?

2. What attitudes have you seen the dark forces sow in your heart to try to divide you from others on the job, in your family, in the church?

3. Why is it so crucial for each of us to be committed to unity in the body of Christ?

4. What does it mean to you personally that you can come to God with freedom, confidence or even boldness?

13   The Prayer

For this reason I kneel before the Father, ¹⁵from whom his whole family in heaven and on earth derives its name. ¹⁶I pray that out of his glorious riches he may strengthen you with power through his Spirit in your inner being, ¹⁷so that Christ may dwell in your hearts through faith. And I pray that you, being rooted and established in love, ¹⁸may have power, together with all the saints, to grasp how wide and long and high and deep is the love of Christ, ¹⁹and to know this love that surpasses knowledge—that you may be filled to the measure of all the fullness of God.

²⁰Now to him who is able to do immeasurably more than all we ask or imagine, according to his power that is at work within us, ²¹to him be glory in the church and in Christ Jesus throughout all generations, for ever and ever! Amen.

Ephesians 3:14-21

With this passionate prayer, we come to the climax of part one of the letter. Paul has given us in the first three chapters a dramatic and powerful view of the plan of God. As we have already noted, writing this was no mere intellectual exercise for Paul. As he writes, he himself is caught up in the words, the concepts and the truth. He had told the story many times, but as he puts these words on paper, he is amazed and awed all over again. His own soul is stirred and his heart is moved to worship. And so he says, "For this reason I kneel before the Father..." (v14). It would not be surprising to learn that Paul stopped his writing and literally got down on his knees to offer this prayer before returning to write it down. Here is something we can be sure of: If the study of these first three chapters does not produce in us an awe of God and his amazing and gracious plan, and a desire to worship and praise him, the message has somehow missed our hearts.

Paul says that he kneels "before the Father, from whom his whole family in heaven and on earth derives its name." What Paul has written about, particularly in chapters 2 and 3, has impressed him with the fact that God has created a new family composed of those from every race, culture and class. Paul glorifies God for being the Father of us all.

For Inner Strength

Much like he did in Ephesians 1, Paul now prays several specific prayers. First he prays that the disciples will be strengthened through the Spirit in their "inner being" (v16). The phrase he uses for this is similar to a phrase used by Plato to describe "the man within." Perhaps the contrast here is with the outward man, who may very well be wasting away (2 Corinthians 4:16-18).

As we grow older, our muscles grow weaker and our strength diminishes. How many fifty-year-olds do you see in the Olympics, the NFL, the NBA or the WNBA? But as we age, we have the capacity to grow stronger in our inner being, and so Paul says in the 2 Corinthians passage, but "inwardly we are being renewed day by day." Because of the work of the Holy Spirit received in our lives by faith, we can become men and women with greater and greater strength within. As I deal with a progressive, chronic disease, I am constantly reminded how crucial it is that I grow stronger in my inner being. I may not have much control over what is happening with the body, but through the Spirit, I can have much control over what happens within. We need to pray for each other what Paul prays for us all, but we need to believe that these prayers can be answered.

For Christ in the Heart

Paul goes on to pray that Christ will dwell in the hearts of believers (v17). The verb he uses is in the present continuous tense. This means his prayer is that Christ will *keep on* dwelling in their hearts more and more. He is praying here for a growing depth of the presence of Christ in the disciples. For Christ to dwell in our hearts means much more than just generating certain feelings in us. The heart stands for all the elements that are the deepest in us. Paul's prayer is that we will be so bonded with Christ that we could never do anything or be in any role without his influence controlling who we are. Is there such a thing as mind control in Christianity? Absolutely. You can read about it in Romans 8:6. However, it is not the control of one person over another, but it is the control of Christ and his Spirit at work in our hearts.

To Grasp the Love

The gospel is a love story with depth. It is no cheap romance novel, but the story of a God who created us, has plans for us and who pursues us in order that he might bless us. In one of the most memorable lines in Ephesians, Paul prays that we might "grasp how wide and long and high and deep is the love of Christ" (v18). Paul knows much will change in our lives if we get a good view of the majestic nature of God's love.

But there is something very important to notice here: His prayer is that this would be done "together with all the saints." It is not surprising to find this in Ephesians, but we should not let it slip by us. Getting a great perspective on the height and breadth of God's love does not come as we isolate ourselves and seek God alone. It comes as we are "together with all the saints." We need each other.

God's plan is to bring us together. In our togetherness we have a much greater opportunity to experience the love of God and to help each other see its richness. I need what you can teach me about God's love, and you need what I can teach you. As we relate to each other, accept each other, help each other and forgive each other, and as we ourselves are "rooted and established in love" (v17), our appreciation and understanding of God's love will grow.

To Be Filled

Paul's final prayer is "that you may be filled to the measure of all the fullness of God" (v19). God has adopted us into his family with the goal of our becoming like him. As amazing as it is, people like us can be filled up with God. No, we will never become perfect images of him in this world, but when we pray Paul's prayer, we can be transformed into God's likeness with ever-increasing glory (2 Corinthians 3:18).

The Grand Finale

The conclusion to Paul's prayer is a reminder of just how much God intends to do with the church. It speaks for itself:

> Now to him who is able to do immeasurably more than all we ask or imagine, according to his power that is at work within us, to him be glory in the church and in Christ Jesus throughout all generations, for ever and ever! Amen. (Ephesians 3:20-21)

Taking Inventory

1. On a scale from 1 to 10, how would you rate your desire to worship and praise God? What does your evaluation reveal?

2. For what challenges and opportunities do you need to gain "strength in your inner being"?

3. What do you consistently do to ensure that Christ is reigning in your heart?

4. Who is someone who has helped you grasp the breadth of God's love?

5. Write out your own commentary on Ephesians 3:20-21, and share with someone what you write.

14 The Life That Is Worthy

> As a prisoner for the Lord, then, I urge you to live a life worthy of the calling you have received. ²Be completely humble and gentle; be patient, bearing with one another in love. ³Make every effort to keep the unity of the Spirit through the bond of peace.
>
> Ephesians 4:1-3

In the first half of Ephesians, Paul very carefully presented some of the most powerful and majestic truths in the great plan of God. Hopefully by this point, we are all standing in awe of the grace and the love of God and the mystery of God that has now been made known. In Ephesians 4 Paul builds on everything he has said in part one of the book, but turns his attention in a different direction. If the first half of the book is designed to help us appreciate what God has done for us, then the second half of the book is designed to call us to live in a way that shows that we appreciate what God has done. So part one is about God's action for us, and part two is about our action in response to God. Part one might be compared to a class we have been in, while part two would then be the test that shows how much we have learned.

What Kind of Life?

The first three chapters of Ephesians show that we have received a calling. God in Christ calls for us to live holy lives and to fulfill his plan. Now Paul urges his readers (including us) to "live a life worthy of the calling" (v1). The statement here is very much like the one we find at a similar point in the Letter to the Romans.

> Therefore, I urge you, brothers, in view of God's
> mercy, to offer your bodies as living sacrifices,
> holy and pleasing to God—this is your spiritual act
> of worship. (Romans 12:1)

God's amazing grace, described again and again in Ephesians 1-3, will have an effect only if we receive it and commit ourselves to live in a way that shows great respect for what God has done for us. God has given us the chance we did not deserve. He has offered the grace we could never earn. Now we must respond. We must be amazed, impressed and awed, and all this must lead us to say, "Love so amazing, so divine, demands my soul, my life, my all!"[1] And let it be clearly said that such a response is not just for a unique and "saintly" few in the church of Christ. It is for every disciple who receives the grace of God. There is a life that fits with how God is blessing us. If we do not want to live the life, we really do not want the grace, for it is designed to produce this new and changed life.

When most people hear about "a life worthy of the calling," they think about a moral lifestyle with a commitment to certain ethical principles. This is certainly part of what Paul has in mind, and he will get to issues related to this matter in Ephesians 5, but in the broader context of Ephesians, it is not surprising that this is not the first thing Paul emphasizes. He actually highlights something to which many religious people do not give a very high priority. The life that Paul considers worthy is a life showing the same passion for unity and relationships that we find in God himself. God's plan has been designed to bring all types of men and women together in one body—the church. The life that is worthy of the calling, then, is first and foremost a life that is committed to keeping disciples united and strong in their relationships.

---

[1] From "When I Survey the Wondrous Cross" by Isaac Watts, 1707.

What Qualities Are Required?

But how do we do this? Paul's answer: "Be completely humble and gentle; be patient, bearing with one another in love" (v2). If anybody should understand how foolish pride is, it should be Christians. If we remember what we were like outside of Christ, if we remind ourselves about how far away from God we were and how enslaved we were by our own sin, we will know that we have no basis for pride and every reason to relate to others with humility.

It's ridiculous how tolerant some of us are of pride in our own lives. It's ugly, it's harmful, but even more, it's stupid. There is absolutely no basis for it. We are all lost apart from the blood of Christ. How absurd it is that we would look down on someone else or act as if we ourselves do not need help. A Christian who has seen his true identity and what God has done for him should "be completely humble" with everyone. Pride is what divides the world. Humility is what brings people together. For us, nothing should make more sense than being completely humble, and no sin should alarm us more than pride. Whenever people are not making progress toward unity, you can be sure of one thing: Someone is not being humble.

If we are humble, we will also be gentle. The word could be translated "meek" and it is a form of the same word Jesus used in the Beatitudes when he said, "Blessed are the meek" (Matthew 5:5). It was a word used by the Greeks to describe a powerful stallion that had been broken and brought under control. To be meek or gentle is to have your passions and emotions brought under control. It is to become teachable and open to input. If we are defensive, irritable, easily angered or full of words with sharp edges, we will alienate others and wound the body of Christ. If we are gentle in spirit, we will bring about reconciliation and healing.

Paul says finally that we must be patient, showing a willingness to bear with each other (hang in there with each other) in love. God has a plan for unity. It will work. The cross brings people together. But we all bring baggage into the kingdom of God. We are all works in progress. We all need to wear signs that say, "Be patient with me; I'm under construction." We have the right goals and dreams, but there will be many issues to resolve to keep the body of Christ united. We must all be committed to hanging in there with each other.

How Much Effort?

In Ephesians 4:3 Paul gives a charge that we need to take with the greatest seriousness. "Make every effort to keep the unity of the Spirit through the bond of peace."

The verb translated "make every effort" carries the idea of diligence and eagerness. Paul is saying that every disciple must show the greatest commitment and diligence to maintaining unity. If unity were easily attained and easily maintained, would such direction have been needed? No, the truth is, unity is fragile. We have the glue needed to keep all of us together, but we must diligently work on our relationships with all the attitudes of heart God calls us to have.

Here then is the message of Ephesians: God says it was worth it to pay the greatest price to bring people of all kinds together in the church. Since this is true, it is right and fitting for all of us to lay down our lives to see that this unity is preserved. One of the saddest and most grievous tragedies you will ever see in the church is when brothers and sisters quickly surrender to disunity. But we see it. We see those who have a disagreement and then leave the fellowship, with no commitment at all to "make every effort to keep the unity." Nothing is more heartbreaking and more hurtful. In Christ, we can work out our conflicts, our tensions and our disagreements. Through humility, gentleness and patience, we can keep loving each other and resolving matters.

Here is what is needed: We need to stand in awe of all that God has done to forgive us and to bring us together in the body of Christ. And then we need to commit ourselves to make every effort to keep the unity of the Spirit—especially when that unity is most threatened or in danger. Jesus said we were worth it. Let's decide that his body is worth it.

Taking Inventory

1. Do your relationships clearly show that God's grace has motivated you to "live a life worthy of the calling"? Have you tolerated pride and allowed it to affect any of your relationships? How?

2. Do others perceive you as thinking you have it all together and do not need help, or do you endear yourself to others and build unity through your humility by getting wise counsel and input for your life?

3. Are you known for gently bringing about resolution and healing in relationships? How can greater humility produce this gentleness in you?

4. Is there anyone with whom you are not completely unified? What further steps can you take to "make every effort" to be unified with that person(s)?

15 The Magnificent Seven

> There is one body and one Spirit—just as you were called to one hope when you were called— ⁵one Lord, one faith, one baptism; ⁶one God and Father of all, who is over all and through all and in all.
>
> Ephesians 4:4-6

Many years ago a man who had some excellent insights into the Scriptures taught me that we make a mistake if we think everything in the Bible is of the same weight. He pointed out that the Pharisees had difficulty distinguishing major issues from minor issues. Not only did they sometimes see minor issues as equal in importance to major ones, but sometimes they even viewed minor issues as being more important. Jesus stressed to them that they needed to emphasize "the more important matters ("weightier matters," KJV) of the law—justice, mercy, and faithfulness" (Matthew 23:23). When we come to this next passage in Ephesians 4, we come to the weightier matters of the kingdom.

We may not always see everything alike (although we must always work to be in agreement), but when it comes to the matters Paul mentions here, we must be absolutely unified. As disciples, all of us have these seven realities in common. Even when we differ on other points, we must "keep the unity" (Ephesians 4:3) because we all share in these.

One Body, One Spirit, One Hope

We can only speculate as to why Paul places these in the order in which he does, but there is no doubt that they made the list because Paul saw each one of them as central to who we are as disciples of Jesus. He first says, "There is one body" (v4), perhaps because this is such a central theme in Ephesians. We must work to keep unity because any two disciples or any two groups of disciples are all part of the *one* body. Jesus certainly did not plan for there to be rival sects, denominations or parties within the community of those who follow him. Everyone who put faith in him and obeyed the gospel was added to the one body, of which Jesus was the one head. Denominational thinking has been common since the days of the Reformation, but it was never God's will.

Each of the three persons of the godhead appears in this list, as we would quite expect, and it is to the "one Spirit" that Paul refers first (v4). Already in this letter he has highlighted the role of the Spirit, who is given to us as an earnest of our inheritance and who has marked us with a seal, showing God's ownership. As Paul said in another letter,

> For we were all baptized by one Spirit into one body—whether Jews or Greeks, slave or free—and we were all given the one Spirit to drink.
> (1 Corinthians 12:13)

The same Spirit who empowers my life, empowers yours. He is the source of spiritual life for us all. How we "grieve the Holy Spirit of God, with whom [we] were sealed for the day of redemption" (Ephesians 4:30) when we allow attitudes of the heart to divide us.

Paul next describes how we were all "called to one hope" when we "were called" (v4). Earlier, in Ephesians 1:18, he prayed that his readers would have the eyes of their hearts opened so that we "may know the hope to which he has called [us], the riches of his glorious inheritance in the saints." We are all headed in the same direction. We will all receive the same glorious inheritance, and it will be "in the saints" — which means it will be along with the saints. We will all be together, and we will all enjoy heaven together. What a powerful motivation to stay united!

One Lord, One Faith, One Baptism

The next three elements Paul mentions might seem more logically to belong at the beginning, but regardless of where they appear in the list, they represent the heart and soul of the Christian experience. There is "one Lord" (v5), and that one Lord is Jesus. The next two items he will mention, faith and baptism, are directly connected to the Lordship of Jesus. "Jesus is Lord" was the confession of the early Christians (Romans 10:9), even when that confession led to persecution, arrest or imprisonment. In Christ we have this in common: we have decided that we cannot manage our own lives and that Jesus needs to become Lord of our attitudes, our actions and our affairs. Whenever two disciples are in conflict and whenever unity is threatened, it changes everything when both realize, "This is not about us, but it is about both of us recognizing that Jesus is Lord and letting him have his way with us."

There is "one faith" (v5). This is not something disconnected from Jesus. When Paul wrote "one Lord, one faith, one baptism," he was describing something that always went together in his mind and in his message. The one faith is not "faith in faith." It is not the virtue of just believing in something, like what you find described in various forms of spirituality today. The one faith here is specifically and only a trust in Jesus and a confidence that he alone deals with our sins and makes us right with God. We need to have the conviction that Paul expressed in Galatians when he said, "The life I live in the body, I live by faith in the Son of God, who loved me and gave himself for me" (Galatians 2:20b). The one faith described here is the link between the one Lord (Jesus) and the one baptism that he describes next.

The fact that baptism makes this list of seven vital elements tells us much about the way it was viewed by the early church and by God himself. According to much tradition, baptism is of minor importance. Many modern commentators will write on a passage like Acts 2:38 and discuss at length repentance, the forgiveness of sins and the gift of the Holy Spirit, but hardly acknowledge that baptism appears in the text. Sometime after the Protestant Reformation, in the wake of Luther's teaching about "faith alone," the idea arose that baptism belonged in the category of works that are done later, having no relationship to salvation. The New Testament writers never saw baptism as some meritorious work that earned anything, but they did see it as the crucial moment when the sinner said to Christ, "I'm lost; I need to die; and I need you to forgive me and raise me up."

Also, as Paul looked at disciples, he knew they all had this in common: they all came into the kingdom in exactly the same way. Everyone entered into Christ by submitting to him in baptism. There was not some "more sophisticated" entrance for the rich and famous. Everyone went humbly down into the water and was raised up to a new life. The "one baptism" was all about the one new birth that brought each person into Christ and into his grace.

One God and Father

Paul concludes his list with the "one" that ties all the others together. There is "one God and Father of all, who is over all and through all and in all" (v6). There is but one God and he is "the God and Father of our Lord Jesus Christ" (Ephesians 1:3). There is nothing in Paul's letter to support the popular notion that all religions should accept one another because they all worship the same God. The one God Paul describes is the God who sent the one Lord Jesus. The New Testament is strong on this point:

> Who is the liar? It is the man who denies that Jesus is the Christ. Such a man is the antichrist—he denies the Father and the Son. No one who denies the Son has the Father; whoever acknowledges the Son has the Father also. (1 John 2:22-23)

In Christ all of us have the same God and Father, the Father of the Son who gave his life for us and the Father who is over everything in our behalf. If he is your Father and he is my Father, and if he is for both of us, how can we not pursue unity?

Whatever the challenges to our relationships, they can be overcome if we hold to the "seven ones" — the weightiest matters in the kingdom.

Taking Inventory

1. Of the "seven ones" mentioned by Paul, which are those about which you have the deepest convictions? Where are your convictions the weakest? (You can determine this one by looking more at how you actually live than by what you think.)

2. If you are united with the other disciples on these seven matters, why will you be able to resolve other differences?

3. Is there anyone in the body of Christ whom you have something against or with whom you have not resolved some matter? How does this passage motivate you to want to change that?

4. Write down one thing you are thankful for in regard to each of the seven matters mentioned by Paul.

16 So the Body May Be Built Up

But to each one of us grace has been given as Christ apportioned it. ⁸This is why it says:

"When he ascended on high,
he led captives in his train
and gave gifts to men."

⁹(What does "he ascended" mean except that he also descended to the lower, earthly regions? ¹⁰He who descended is the very one who ascended higher than all the heavens, in order to fill the whole universe.) ¹¹It was he who gave some to be apostles, some to be prophets, some to be evangelists, and some to be pastors and teachers, ¹²to prepare God's people for works of service, so that the body of Christ may be built up ¹³until we all reach unity in the faith and in the knowledge of the Son of God and become mature, attaining to the whole measure of the fullness of Christ.

¹⁴Then we will no longer be infants, tossed back and forth by the waves, and blown here and there by every wind of teaching and by the cunning and craftiness of men in their deceitful scheming. ¹⁵Instead, speaking the truth in love, we will in all things grow up into him who is the Head, that is, Christ. ¹⁶From him the whole body, joined and held together by every supporting ligament, grows and builds itself up in love, as each part does its work.

Ephesians 4:7-16

The church is the body of Christ. God, in his plan, has chosen to use the church to carry on the work of Christ. As Jesus himself was God in the flesh, the church is the presence of the divine Christ in a human flesh and blood community. As a human community with a divine mission, the church is like any community in that it must have leadership. Those naive folks who want their religion without having anyone in a leadership role are out of touch with both experience and with the teachings of Scripture. Certainly people have reasons to be skeptical of leadership. There have been abuses in religion just as there have been in other realms. But when the church is doing what pleases God, it will be because godly leadership is being provided and followed.

Where Leaders Lead

Paul begins this section by noting that we have all been given gifts, in just the way that Christ wanted to give them. This is important to understand and believe. Every disciple is useful and needed. But Paul highlights certain leadership gifts that are given, because none of us will be able to use our gifts most effectively if the body of Christ is without direction. The apostles, prophets, evangelists and pastor/teachers (v11) are the ones who give it that direction. The work of the inspired apostles and prophets was completed in the first century, but now evangelists and elders ("pastor" is another word for "shepherd") are to anchor themselves in the Scriptures provided by the apostles and prophets (Ephesians 2:20) and then guide the church to fulfill those scriptures.

It is not the role of leaders to do all the work—that would be impossible! Their role is "to prepare God's people for works of service," with the goal of building up the body of Christ (Ephesians 4:12). There is an important idea here. The body of Christ is built up when all the members of the body are prepared to contribute and when all use their gifts and their abilities to serve others. To build a strong and healthy church, leaders must do more than give direction and set up accountability. They must do what is needed "to prepare" disciples to use their different gifts. The New American Standard Bible uses the phrase "equipping of the saints for the work of service."

However, as leaders do this, there is something else that they are to focus on: helping all to reach unity in the faith and maturity in Christ (v13). The way this verse reads ("until we all attain to the unity," NASB) seems to imply that unity does not exist just because you put a group of Christians together. It is something we move toward and arrive at only as leaders prepare people to use their gifts. In the same way, maturity in Christ is a goal to be sought. Maturity, by its very nature, is not something that is bestowed on us, but something that comes over time as we practice what we are taught (see Hebrews 5:14). Note that unity and maturity go hand in hand. You do not have one without the other.

What can we conclude from Paul's words about leadership? We must see leadership as vital to the church. We must not think that leaders have more value than others (for everyone is valuable); but we must recognize how essential it is for leaders to carry out their work. Certainly implied in what Paul says is the idea stated clearly by the writer of Hebrews, that we should obey our leaders and make their work a joy and not a burden (Hebrews 13:17). When leaders don't lead as they should, their failures must be addressed; but when leadership fails, we must not overreact and throw out the baby with the bathwater. Strong leadership is essential to the body of Christ and must always be supported.

And Everyone Grows Up

Having mentioned the goal of maturity, Paul turns more specifically to this theme in verse 14 of Ephesians 4. When leaders fulfill the role God has for them, the result will be that people will mature and will "no longer be infants" who are vulnerable to the latest novel ideas that come along. Thus, a key role of leaders is to make sure that people have adequate opportunities to study the Scriptures and become grounded in Biblical truth.

A key to growth is stated clearly in verse 15, "Instead, speaking the truth in love, we will in all things grow up into him who is the Head, that is, Christ." Maturity develops over time, but it will not develop, even with time, unless we are involved in each others' lives and unless we are bringing two vital elements to each other: truth and love. Truth, as already pointed out, comes from the message of the apostles and prophets—from the Scriptures. We must not just hang out together and enjoy one another's company. We must bring each other the truth—but we must always do this with love. Truth can be brought in harsh, cold ways, without feeling or empathy. But the truth causes us to grow when someone brings it with the love that makes us feel cared for, believed in and supported.

And here is a vital point: We all need to speak the truth in love to others, and we all need the truth spoken in love to us. No one is so mature that he doesn't need the perspective and help of others. No one is so in touch with his own life that he cannot benefit from the insights of others into his actions and attitudes. Leaders, especially with their important role of guiding God's people, need to see their ongoing need for this kind of help. It's dangerous indeed for anyone to think they no longer need the counsel and help of others.

This section concludes with Paul reminding us that the church is truly like a body that is "joined and held together by every supporting ligament" (v16). The only hope for us spiritually is to stay together and to stay connected. Our relationships are these ligaments, holding all the different parts together and enabling each part to really do its work in the most edifying way. I have one set of gifts; you have another. As we stay connected and united, my gifts and yours can be fully used and complement each other. And this must be our standard: *Each part does its work.*

Years ago I read about the 80/20 rule, which says that eighty percent of the work of any organization is usually done by twenty percent of the people. It has been disturbing to see this trend make its way into our churches in recent years. We must all have a conviction that we will not allow this to be true of the church, for in the church, each individual part must strive to do its work. Only then will the body be able to show the world Christ who is her head.

Taking Inventory

1. What gifts and abilities are you currently using to contribute to the needs around you in the body of Christ? List them.

2. As a leader or future leader, what can you do to better prepare the disciples around you for "works of service" and to meet one another's needs?

3. What can you change in order to be more of a joy to your leaders?

4. Regardless of your role(s) in the church, how often do you actually open the Bible with another disciple in order to bring each other the truth in love? Can you build this into the times you already have scheduled this week with other disciples?

17 Made New

So I tell you this, and insist on it in the Lord, that you must no longer live as the Gentiles do, in the futility of their thinking. [18]They are darkened in their understanding and separated from the life of God because of the ignorance that is in them due to the hardening of their hearts. [19]Having lost all sensitivity, they have given themselves over to sensuality so as to indulge in every kind of impurity, with a continual lust for more.

[20]You, however, did not come to know Christ that way. [21]Surely you heard of him and were taught in him in accordance with the truth that is in Jesus. [22]You were taught, with regard to your former way of life, to put off your old self, which is being corrupted by its deceitful desires; [23]to be made new in the attitude of your minds; [24]and to put on the new self, created to be like God in true righteousness and holiness.

Ephesians 4:17-24

Paul has made it exceedingly clear that we are saved by grace, but those who are saved by grace are called to say "No" to an old life and "Yes" to a new life. Grace covers sin, but grace is no license *to* sin. Grace teaches us to change our lives (Titus 2:11-12). To accept grace and then return to the old life makes as much sense as getting a cure for cancer and then purposefully stepping in front of an oncoming train. Grace is given to rescue us, to bring us out of an empty life, to keep us on a new path. There is nothing tepid about Paul's language here. He is passionate about the strong response we must make to God's call.

Putting Off the Old

Paul is clear as to why the old life must be totally renounced. In 4:17-19 he uses some powerfully descriptive phrases to characterize life outside of Christ. First, he says it is a life of futile thinking (v17). Unspiritual people, who live by their own rules, still engage in thinking, but because they do not focus on God or his word, in the end their thinking will all be futile. At times it may be obviously foolish. However, in the short run it may sometimes be impressive. It may result in some artistic, political or financial success or recognition. It may bring pleasure. But in the end, if it is not connected to God and his ultimate purpose, all such thinking will all come to nothing. We must remember this when we are tempted to be impressed by man's accomplishments.

Those in the world are "darkened in their understanding" because they are "separated from the life of God" (v18). Because they do not look at life through God's eyes, they do not understand who they are or what life is about. What is more, they cannot claim to be innocent victims. Their ignorance is due to "the hardening of their hearts" (v18). They have turned their backs on the knowledge of God.

Paul's next sentence sounds like a description written after a trip through modern culture. "Having lost all sensitivity, they have given themselves over to sensuality so as to indulge in every kind of impurity, with a continual lust for more" (v19). Just a few minutes of channel surfing or a quick read about what is available on the Internet is all that's needed for us to see how much of the world is caught up in the very thing Paul describes. Few inhibitions remain. Few standards are held. Music, television, movies, books and Web sites encourage people to indulge every desire. Our children grow up in an environment saturated with sensuality. The hallmark of this way of life is self-centeredness. People make their own rules to satisfy their own desires. Acknowledging a holy God and seeking to obey him is not on their agenda.

Putting On the New

Disciples must have nothing to do with such a self-indulgent lifestyle. As Paul said to the Romans, "What shall we say, then? Shall we go on sinning so that grace may increase? By no means! We died to sin; how can we live in it any longer?" (Romans 6:1-2).

The old life is not one we learned from Christ (v20). On the contrary, when we were taught about him and saw the truth as it was lived out in the man Jesus (v21), it was the total opposite of the spirit that we had seen in the world. Jesus said, the world "hates me because I testify that what it does is evil" (John 7:7).

Paul reminds the disciples that when they were taught about Jesus, they were shown that following him would be an end to a former way of life (v22). There was no way they could come into God's kingdom and continue in a way of life opposed to God. They were clearly taught that following Jesus meant putting off the old self because it was "being corrupted by its deceitful desires." The word for "desires" here is *epithumia*, which carries with it, especially in a context like this one, the idea of a life with self at the center.

As the believers read this from Paul, surely they remembered the central message of discipleship that they had been taught:

> "If anyone would come after me, he must deny himself and take up his cross daily and follow me. For whoever wants to save his life will lose it, but whoever loses his life for me will save it." (Luke 9:23-24)

It has been well said that Jesus calls a man to come and die. No one follows Jesus without a radical decision to end one way of life and begin a new one. Paul is reminding all disciples that this decision must be remembered and consistently reaffirmed. As Jesus said, it must be a decision that we make *daily*.

The world will constantly be influencing us to return to its message. Motivated by grace, we must just as constantly reject the old life and remember why it is not for us.

You were taught, says Paul, "to be made new in the attitude of your minds; and to put on the new self, created to be like God in true righteousness and holiness" (vv23-24). Everything starts with a change of mind. We must realize that our own thinking is futile and will not lead to the fulfillment of God's purposes. If we follow it, we will miss the whole point of our lives. So we put something "new" in our minds—at least something new to us: God's thinking. As we will see in the next chapter of Ephesians, our goal as disciples is not to figure out what we think is best, but to "find out what pleases the Lord" (Ephesians 5:10).

This leads to putting on a new self—to actually becoming a different person—a person who wants to think like God and live like God. Paul talks about being like God "in true righteousness and holiness" (v24). Righteousness in the Scriptures is primarily about how we treat other people and how we conduct relationships. Therefore Paul will deal with various aspects of relationships in the rest of this chapter.[1] Holiness is all about understanding that we are set apart for a purpose and then living in a way which fulfills that purpose.

We live in an irreverent world, where one of the core beliefs is that nothing is sacred. Disciples were not taught this in Jesus. No, we were taught that God's message is sacred, to be respected and to be treasured in our hearts and minds. We were taught that our very lives are sacred and are to be lived for God and in line with his truth. This is not just a different life. It's the *new* life and the only life that is not futile.

---

[1] See an excellent article, "Religious or Righteous," on this subject by Fred Faller in *The Leader's Resource Handbook* (Woburn, Mass.: DPI, 1998), 143.

Taking Inventory

1. Do you have a deep conviction that the way of Jesus and the way of the world are opposites? Do you share his conviction that what the world does is evil? How does your conviction show up in your actions?

2. What temptations do you face as you make choices concerning which movies and television programs you will watch, the music you will listen to and the Web sites that you will visit? Do your choices reflect your "new" life in Christ?

3. In what ways has your thinking changed the most since you became a disciple of Jesus? What new perspectives are you most thankful for?

18 Right and Wrong

> Therefore each of you must put off falsehood and speak truthfully to his neighbor, for we are all members of one body. [26]"In your anger do not sin": Do not let the sun go down while you are still angry, [27]and do not give the devil a foothold. [28]He who has been stealing must steal no longer, but must work, doing something useful with his own hands, that he may have something to share with those in need.
>
> Ephesians 4:25-28

A major problem with much so-called spirituality is that it never gets practical—which is not true of Biblical spirituality. Having described in general terms a new life that Christians have entered, Paul now makes various practical points about how our new outlook is to affect our relationships with others. We may talk with eloquence about finding God, but why should anyone listen if it does not have a major effect on the way we treat those around us? We do not get into Christ by keeping a law—any law—but once we have submitted ourselves to the Lordship of Christ, we are people who must live under Christ's law (1 Corinthians 9:21). There are certain things that are always right and other things that are always wrong. As disciples of Jesus, we must be totally committed to this outlook. If there is moral ambiguity in our lives, the gospel of Jesus will be tarnished.

A Corrupt Generation

In the world it is common for people to lie to each other, to become bitterly angry with each other, and to take advantage

95

of each other to fulfill their own desires. Such behavior is everywhere around us. Presidents look into TV cameras and lie. Husbands lie to their wives, wives to their husbands, and children lie to their parents and teachers. Doctors and CEOs have restraining orders taken out against them because of their anger and rage. Parents and children mutually threaten each other. As I write this chapter, twenty-four football players from a Big Ten university have just been suspended for stealing from a shoe store. Today's headlines also describe a twenty-two-year-old college student just arrested for using the Internet to make $250,000 in a fraudulent stock trade.

To follow Jesus is much more than a commitment to ethics and morality, but no one follows Jesus without a strong commitment to his radical ethics and his radical morality.

Lying

Disciples of Jesus must put off falsehood. Since most of us came from a world where lying was tolerated, we must certainly put off what we once had on. Whereas we once used lying to make ourselves look better, to avoid something unpleasant or to get something we wanted, we must now put this behavior away completely and speak truthfully with our neighbor. Such truthfulness may result in temporary discomfort or inconvenience—or even some long-term pain—but what will a man give in exchange for his integrity? Those who lie try to take life into their own hands and show no trust in God. Lying is wrong and sinful. We must have nothing to do with it.

Rage

Disciples of Jesus must control anger. Hopefully those who read this book ten years from now will have no idea what WWF stands for, but at this writing, the World Wrestling Federation programs draw more viewers in the eighteen to thirty-four age range than any other TV programs. In these televised "matches," men (and now women) threaten to destroy each other, scream insults and vulgarities at each other, and even smash each other with chairs and other objects. All of this is, of course, scripted and, to some extent, controlled; but in this theater of the absurd, anger and violence are celebrated, and no doubt, encouraged. Christians must not buy into this culture. It is not wrong to become angry, but it's wrong to let anger control us. It's wrong for it to cause us to treat someone else sinfully. And it is definitely wrong for anger to turn into bitterness or rage (v31).

In this context, Paul gives us the most practical of admonitions: "Do not let the sun go down while you are still angry, and do not give the devil a foothold" (vv26-27). When something bothers us and hurts us and stirs up anger within us, we must deal with it quickly. We must talk it out, pray through it and resolve it. Anger left until another day is only bigger the next time you see it, and the bigger it gets, the more the enemy is able to use it.

Stealing

Disciples of Jesus must no longer steal, but instead, they must serve. Stealing is universally recognized as wrong and punishable by law in every culture, but do we understand what is so wrong with it? Sure, there would be chaos if stealing were accepted, but there's a deeper reason. God teaches us to respect others and to focus on giving, not taking. This is why it's not enough for a Christian to not steal. No, we must work hard to earn money righteously, so that we can share with others who are in need — *not* so that we can buy all the latest toys! If you are looking for a verse to support a savings account, see verse 28. How can we be ready to help others in their time of need unless we have put money away, not only for the unexpected events in our own lives, but in the lives of others as well?

A Christian approach to ethics is more than technical adherence to the law. A Christian approach says, "I want to treat people as Jesus treated them." A Christian approach recognizes that certain things are wrong and absolutely refuses to be involved in those, but it goes further. It says, "I am here to put others first, to treat them with respect and to meet their needs as I trust God to meet mine."

Taking Inventory

1. Which of the three areas discussed here are the most tempting to you? What do you do to guard yourself?

2. What personal experience causes you to have conviction about not letting the sun go down while you are still angry?

3. What are you doing to prepare to meet the unexpected needs of others?

19 Building Others Up

Do not let any unwholesome talk come out of your mouths, but only what is helpful for building others up according to their needs, that it may benefit those who listen. [30]And do not grieve the Holy Spirit of God, with whom you were sealed for the day of redemption. [31]Get rid of all bitterness, rage and anger, brawling and slander, along with every form of malice. [32]Be kind and compassionate to one another, forgiving each other, just as in Christ God forgave you.

Ephesians 4:29-32

Shortly we will come to Ephesians 5 where we will be told that we must live a life of love. But what does it mean to really love people? That's what this passage is all about: treating each other with respect and relating to each other just as God in Christ relates to us. It is about considering others and caring about how our attitudes, words and actions affect them. The immature person thinks very little about the impact his actions have on others. The mature, spiritual man or woman is concerned that what he or she does helps others to grow and be encouraged.

Watch Your Mouth

When we think of the problem of abuse, we usually think first of someone who physically harms or violates another person. However, the most common form of abuse is probably verbal. So much of what comes out of people's mouths tears down, demeans, traumatizes, discourages or brings despair. "The tongue also is a fire, a world of evil among the parts of the body," says James (3:6); "it corrupts the whole person, sets the whole course of his life on fire, and is itself set on fire by hell." With our tongues we can bring hell to the lives of others. We can rob them of encouragement, hope and joy. With our tongues we can tear down faith and bring sinister glee to the demons who see people being driven in their direction.

And so the first thing Paul says here is to think about your words. Do not let things come out of your mouth that hurt people (v29), that is, things that diminish their faith, hope or love. The word for "unwholesome" here is *sapros*, which means rotten or worthless. It is communication that has absolutely no value. It helps no one. It can only do damage. Too many of us just open our mouths and selfishly let things flow out without regard for what those words are doing to someone else. A few of us may naively think that words aren't that potent.

Husbands, we are guilty of rotten talk when we make our wives feel like failures or as if they have no value. Parents, we are guilty of worthless talk when we have no words for our children that build them up and make them thankful for who they are. Disciples, we are guilty of unwholesome talk when we critique another's life, but offer no words of hope or grace. Leaders, our words do harm, not good, when they come from our own frustration and not from hearts that care for people.

Certainly some destructive talk is calculated and premeditated. It is spoken deliberately to cause hurt. However, most of our unwholesome talk comes because we just do not stop and consider what the other person needs in order to be built up. We are so eager to vent our own feelings that we do not even think about what our spouses or children or friends need from us. When we speak from our own frustration, anger or disappointment, without concern for what our words will do to another person, we have come down from the cross and gone back to living by the flesh. So when your words are consistently unwholesome, it is not enough to merely try to discipline your tongue. You must see your heart and how far you have wandered from the cross, for it is out of the overflow of the heart that the mouth speaks (Luke 6:45).

When we hurt others with our talk, the Holy Spirit that lives in us is grieved (v30). The word for "grieve" is *lupeo*, which means to distress, to cause grief or heaviness. Surely with tears the Spirit says to us, "That's not why I am here. I am the Comforter, not the one who harms" (see John 14:26 KJV).

All of this, of course, is inconsistent with the truth that is in Jesus (v22) and the new life we have found through him (v24). Therefore, it is time that we commit ourselves whole-heartedly to changing our hearts and desiring to speak only words that build others up and meet their needs.[1]

Fix Your Eyes on Christ

In one sense bitterness (v31) can be said to be like cancer. It eats away at the person who is filled with it. It sucks the joy and love out of his soul. But cancer may not be the best analogy, because while cancer is not contagious, bitterness most certainly is.

The writer of Hebrews recognizes how bitterness moves rapidly from heart to heart when he writes, "See to it that no one misses the grace of God and that no bitter root grows up to cause trouble and defile many" (Hebrews 12:15). The word used for "bitterness" is *pikria*, which can also mean poison. In the body of Christ, that is exactly what bitterness is. It poisons and defiles the whole body. Get ten joyful Christians together, bring one bitter person in among them, and watch how this one can pull the others down and suck the life out of the group. And as the writer of Hebrews points out, it only takes a *root* of bitterness to do damage, because a bitter root always grows. And this may be why Paul says,

---

[1] There is one time when we need to let all the ugly stuff in our hearts come out, specifically when someone is with us to help us to deal with it and overcome it. Most of the time we cannot be healed until we get all the bile out one last time. However, you need to do this with a mature disciple who is listening for the expressed purpose of helping you be free from whatever has caused these strong emotions.

"Get rid of all bitterness," because even in its incipient form, it is a spiritual arsenic that will destroy both the carrier and those whom he defiles.

In my observation, bitterness is one of the greatest dangers for disciples. We may have dealt with the outward sins, but after some disappointments in the church, some pain caused by someone else's lack of consideration, or because of some dream that was dashed, the root of bitterness can appear. Perhaps at first it is almost microscopic in form, but that's all it takes. No matter how small its beginning, bitterness will grow if we do not deal with it. We may still be reading our Bibles, still praying, still seen in the fellowship. We may even still be reaching out to the lost. But something insidious is happening. The body of Christ is slowly being poisoned. This is no minor matter. It is the most serious of sins, and this is why Paul says to "get rid of it all." We must get down to the very roots of it and rid our hearts of it completely.

Ironically, but also quite logically, bitter people can be very self-righteous people at the same time. Though guilty of bringing poison into the body of Christ, they believe that they are right and others are wrong. They think that they are justified in their bitterness. Not only do they sin, but they vigorously defend their right to continue in their sin.

But here is what Paul would have us understand: No matter what has been done to you by men in the world or in the church, that which God in Christ has done for you is so good and so great that no harm you could undergo on earth could ever diminish it.

When we are bitter or angry, or full of rage or malice, we are not standing at the foot of the cross with eyes fixed on Christ. We are focused on ourselves and on what others have done to us. The first step is always to be convicted of our ingratitude. The solution is always to come back to the cross and to fix our eyes on what God in Christ has done for us. With this clear and fresh in our minds, we will then be ready to be kind and compassionate to others (all others) and to forgive just as we have been so richly and freely forgiven. As a result grace, not poison, will spread through the body of Christ, making it healthy and strong.

Taking Inventory

1. Ask someone who is spiritually strong and someone who is not as strong how they feel about the words that come out of your mouth. If they report to you that they hear unwholesome talk, search for the root of it.

2. If you are married or live within a family, find out how others in the family feel about what comes out of your mouth. Even ask your young children. Again, search for the roots of any problems.

3. Write down the names of three people (but not all in your family) that you can build up in the body of Christ. Think through the words that you will use.

4. Be very honest about this: Is there even a small root of bitterness in you about anything? Do you believe that it's a poison? Will you talk with someone about it immediately?

5. How does it change the way you relate to others when you stand at the foot of the cross?

20 Love Life

Be imitators of God, therefore, as dearly loved children ²and live a life of love, just as Christ loved us and gave himself up for us as a fragrant offering and sacrifice to God.

Ephesians 5:1-2

In many ways the first two verses of Ephesians 5 sum up the last part of chapter 4 and the rest of chapter 5. Living the new life in Christ is all about living a life of love. The word for love here is *agape*, the one word for love in the Greek language that meant unconditional commitment. The Greeks had other words for love including *eros*, which referred to romantic love; *storge*, which referred to family love; and *philia*, which referred to brotherly kindness or friendship love. *Agape* is unique in that it refers to a love that we have for others, not because they can give us satisfaction in some way, but because of a commitment we make to them that is completely unconditional.

Imitators of God

Certainly the imitation of God in many areas is simply not possible for us. I can no more imitate God's omnipresence or his omniscience than I can imitate his creative power. But we *can* imitate God's love. We can learn to be committed unconditionally to others just as he has been unconditionally committed to us. His Holy Spirit is in us to produce this very fruit.

The word *agape* was not widely used or discussed prior to the coming of Jesus. But it became the predominant word for Christian love because from Christ we have learned to be devoted not only to those closest to us, but to those who are enemies (Matthew 5:44, Luke 6:27, 35), and thus to everyone in between. *Agape* by its very unconditional nature can make no distinction. Our love must fall like the rain on the righteous and the unrighteous (Matthew 5:45).

On the day I wrote this chapter I read of a family in Canada that experienced the brutal murder of two of their children. Shortly after this terrible event they were introduced to disciples and to the message of Jesus. As they became his followers, they found the power and inspiration to do what many people would think impossible. They were able to commit themselves to the welfare of the killer. Even in the face of their devastating loss, which would have left most people deeply embittered and calling for revenge, they found that the imitation of Christ led them to put away their anger so that they could love the guilty man and pray for his salvation. (And some of us have trouble loving a brother who did not speak to us warmly!) There is no doubt that this family saw the heart of God and determined, in the face of life's most challenging circumstances, that they would imitate that heart. God's great plan as revealed in Ephesians is not simply for us to be good church members, but to become like him in the way we think and the way we act.

On more than one occasion I have had disciples tell me that they are not finding their Christian walk to be very exciting. This says more about their hearts than it does about the Christian walk. What can be more exciting than learning to be like God? What can be more stimulating than allowing his Holy Spirit to work in us so that we become devoted to people and care for people just as he does? In a passage known to almost everyone, Paul wrote about faith, hope and love (*agape*), and concluded that the greatest of these is love (1 Corinthians 13:13). What can be more fulfilling than to become skillful in doing the greatest thing in the world?

Imitators of Christ

The Old Testament shows us a God of love. The never-ending nature of his love is described in many passages like this one found both in 1 Chronicles 16:34 and Psalm 106:1:

> Give thanks to the Lord, for he is good;
> his love endures forever.

The breadth of God's love is described in passages like this one in Psalm 103:11:

> For as high as the heavens are above the earth,
> so great is his love for those who fear him.

But as great as Old Testament statements are about God's love, it was not until Jesus went to the cross that we saw how wide and long and high and deep his love really is (Ephesians 3:18). Now, for those of us who live this side of the cross, the phrase "just as Christ loved us" compels us to take love to new levels every day.

Your spouse committed a thoughtless act. Maybe your spouse did something even more hurtful that deeply wounded your marriage. How do you respond? *"Just as Christ loved us."*

Your child did something that embarrassed you, hurt you and discouraged you. How do you respond? *"Just as Christ loved us."*

Your parents put you down and left you feeling that you can never please them. Maybe they did something bad that you would have never thought they would do. What truth should you rely on now? *"Just as Christ loved us."*

Your neighbor or your coworker misrepresented you to others. How will you now treat them? *"Just as Christ loved us."*

Your brother or sister in Christ did not encourage you. Maybe this disciple was even harsh with you. Maybe he or she overlooked you for some role in favor of someone less capable. What principle will you follow now? *"Just as Christ loved us."*

You spent hours with a fellow disciple trying to help him or her change. The person then went and acted foolishly, completely ignoring the counsel you gave from the Scriptures. What phrase do you most need to focus on the next time you are with him or her? *"Just as Christ loved us."*

Over the years I have seen remarkable things happen when disciples have truly been disciples and have decided that "just as Christ loved us" would be the guiding rule of their lives. I have seen wives keep on loving their husbands even after years of painful interactions. I have seen deeply scarred children forgive parents for neglect and abuse. I have seen brothers in Christ develop a deep relationship after feeling distance and tension. I have seen Christians return good for evil and show love and concern to those who persecuted them and maligned them. I have seen disciples who were abandoned by their spouses get rid of all bitterness and pray continuously that those who left would return to God.

To commit ourselves to go through life "just as Christ loved us" will not mean a cheery life, free of pain. On the contrary, "as Christ loved us" will mean that we will go the way of suffering. What especially distinguishes *agape* love from all other "loves" is that it accepts the fact that pain is a part of love and that true love only is demonstrated as we maintain it through our pain.

Years ago I read a comment based on Luke 9:51. There Luke tells us, "As the time approached for him to be taken up to heaven, Jesus resolutely set out for Jerusalem." Reflecting on the fact that Jesus knew very well what awaited him in that city, the author stated simply,

Jesus leaned into his pain.

Jesus clearly showed us what God had been doing all along—facing pain for us. But in Jesus we see that God does not love us by sitting on the sidelines and shouting, "I love you." No, he enters into our suffering and bears burdens we could not bear. This is not because we deserve for him to do this. It is an act of pure grace. And now we are called to go into the hard places and live among others "just as Christ loved us."

Taking Inventory

1. Would people say that you are active in your church or that you truly live a life of love?

2. What do you need to change in order to have the reputation for living a life of love?

3. List three situations in which you need to focus on the phrase "just as Christ loved us."

4. What does the imitation of Christ's love teach you about pain?

21   Rejecting the Darkness

But among you there must not be even a hint of sexual immorality, or of any kind of impurity, or of greed, because these are improper for God's holy people. ⁴Nor should there be obscenity, foolish talk or coarse joking, which are out of place, but rather thanksgiving. ⁵For of this you can be sure: No immoral, impure or greedy person—such a man is an idolater—has any inheritance in the kingdom of Christ and of God. ⁶Let no one deceive you with empty words, for because of such things God's wrath comes on those who are disobedient. ⁷Therefore do not be partners with them.

Ephesians 5:3-7

Biblical faith is not legalistic. The Bible does not teach that by being morally good, keeping all the rules, you can be saved. Hopefully at this point in our study of Ephesians, it is clear that salvation is by grace. Hopefully this is a deep conviction in our lives. But as Paul would write later in another letter:

For the grace of God that brings salvation has appeared to all men. It teaches us to say "No" to ungodliness and worldly passions, and to live self-controlled, upright and godly lives in this present age. (Titus 2:11-12)

We simply are not serious about receiving God's grace if we are not serious about letting grace do its work, and the work of grace is to make us righteous and to teach us to say "No" to the darkness. Many who wear the name of Jesus proclaim a grace that makes excuses instead of a grace that transforms. Paul makes it clear in this passage that the person who receives God's grace must just as surely embrace God's call to live a different life.

Sexual Ethics

In the last few centuries we have seen an ever-increasing loosening of sexual morals. Sexual immorality, as defined by the Bible, completely dominates our culture. The vast majority of references to sexual activity on television shows and in movies are references to sex outside of marriage. Among consenting adults, the only sexual practice condemned by our society would seem to be the practice of having "unprotected" sex when you know you have the HIV infection. Of course, to oppose homosexuality is to be homophobic and extremely politically incorrect.

Coarse joking (v4) is the heart and soul of modern comedy. It is almost impossible to find a comedian who does not make constant reference to sexual activity outside of marriage. The most popular sitcoms of our day are built around this theme, and few writers dare deviate from it. Our culture is obsessed with sex, and when we think things cannot go much further, someone pushes the envelope and shocks us all over again. The dark fruits of divorce, abortion, STDs and sexual addiction, not to mention personal emptiness, are showing that there is most certainly a price to pay for this rewriting of all the rules—but as always, people are slow to learn.

The Bible does not avoid the subject of sex. Sex is not a creation of Satan, but the gift of a good and loving God. Like all God's gifts, it is intended to bless his people, and when used in a godly fashion within the marriage relationship, it does richly bless. A number of years ago it occurred to me that alongside the teleological argument, the cosmological argument and the ontological argument for God's existence, we may need to add the sexual argument. I am not sure that philosophers will see it on a par with these other traditional arguments. However, the power of sexuality to give us remarkable pleasure while it deepens the bond between a husband and a wife who are committed to each other is an indication that there is a loving Gift-Giver behind this universe. Why else would women have an organ that has no other purpose but to give intense sexual pleasure?

But while the Bible teaches that sex is good, it also teaches that we can misuse it and abuse it and do with it that which violates God's great plan for us. As the gospel came into a culture not unlike ours, where there were very few restrictions on sexual practice, Paul was extremely clear: Among disciples, there must not be even a hint of sexual immorality or impurity. We must totally reject the world's lack of standards and totally embrace God's standards. The temptations will be powerful and they will be pervasive, but they must be rejected for one main reason: *We are God's holy people*—a people set apart for a unique purpose. We must experience God's gift of sex only within the bounds of his gracious will and never think that we have the right to fulfill our desires according to our own plans. When we became disciples, we gave up that "me centered" approach.

What the world does with sex may be found in *every place* you turn, but as far as God is concerned, it is *out of place* (v4). It does not belong in his plan, and his people must reject the world and refuse to be partners with those in it, whether in word or deed. Will we be ridiculed for our commitment? Of course. Does that matter? Not at all. Whatever price we must pay to be faithful to God and his truth is worth it.

Material Ethics

Most of us read the passage above, and we hear rather clearly the call to sexual purity. But there is something else in this passage. It calls us just as strongly to reject greed. We must no more dabble with greed than with sexual sin (v3). The person with a greedy heart has no more place in the kingdom of God than does an impure person (v5). Among Christians, this is not addressed nearly as often as the issue of sexual impurity, but God sees no difference.[1]

Perhaps we have more trouble with greed because it is more difficult to define. The Greek word here is *pleonexia*, which is translated "covetousness" in the King James Version. Certainly either word refers to our desire to have something more than what we need or to have something that others have. Like sexual immorality, it is rooted in selfishness. Like sexual immorality, it is blind to the needs of others, and it blocks our ability to love people in an unconditional way. Like sexual immorality, greed involves god-playing—the thinking that if life is going to be full, we will have to do it our way and get what we want. Paul says clearly that the greedy person is an idolater (v5). He sets something else in the place of God, and "gain" (the desire for more) becomes his true god.

Most people think they know greedy people but do not think of themselves as greedy. Even when we are being greedy, most of us are oblivious to our condition and are quick to offer a defense for our purchases and desires. For this reason, we need others in our lives who will ask us tough questions, call us to personal sacrifice, and speak up whenever they wonder if we are heading down the road of greed. Because greed is more difficult to define, we may need to be even more vigilant and prayerful about putting it away. It is a blight on the spiritual life.

As we saw in the last chapter, the goal for the new man or woman in Christ is to live a life of love. We can have nothing to do with sexual impurity and greed because both lead us away from *agape* love and away from the plan of God.

---

[1] On this topic I highly recommend to all disciples Douglas Jacoby's chapter, "The Spirit of the West: The Curse of Consumerism," in his book *The Spirit* (Woburn, Mass.: DPI, 1998).

Taking Inventory

1. Even when we are fully convinced that the sexual attraction offered by the world has no real value, we can still be tempted. What are the greatest challenges for you?

2. In the last six months have you been completely open with another Christian about where your own mind and heart are in regard to sexual thoughts and feelings? Have you been honest about any sexual sin?

3. If you have children who are elementary school age or older, what are you teaching them about God's plan for sex? Do they understand the wonder and beauty of it, as well as the need to use it only God's way?

4. Who would be the very best person to help you evaluate the possibility of greed in your life?

5. What helps you to be content with what you have?

22 As Children of Light

For you were once darkness, but now you are light in the Lord. Live as children of light ⁹(for the fruit of the light consists in all goodness, righteousness and truth) ¹⁰and find out what pleases the Lord. ¹¹Have nothing to do with the fruitless deeds of darkness, but rather expose them. ¹²For it is shameful even to mention what the disobedient do in secret. ¹³But everything exposed by the light becomes visible, ¹⁴for it is light that makes everything visible. This is why it is said:

"Wake up, O sleeper,
    rise from the dead,
and Christ will shine on you."

Ephesians 5:8-14

To the first century outsider observing a Christian baptism, it may have appeared to be just another initiation ceremony among the many that were found in various religious groups. However, to the person being baptized, it was clearly the beginning of a totally new life. A baptism in the first century would have most likely been done outdoors. Frequently the person would exchange his old clothes for a white robe for the baptism. Singing was a vital part of the early Christians' experience, as Paul will describe shortly (v19). As a convert emerged from the water of baptism, feeling a great sense of joy, he or she would have been greeted by happy people, who usually would have had a song on their lips.

It is suggested by many scholars that what we have in verse 14 is a fragment of an early Christian hymn, most likely one that was a favorite at baptismal services. Having been taught that in baptism our old life dies and we are raised to a new life, the disciple would have heard his family in Christ exhorting him and encouraging him with these words:

> "Wake up, O sleeper,
>   rise from the dead,
> and Christ will shine on you."

He who had been dead in sin could now wake up and rise to a new life because Christ would be shining his life-giving light on him. In those simple words the convert heard a profound message: You are new. You don't have to live the old way anymore. A powerful presence is now in your life.

Once Darkness, Now Light

Paul again reminds his readers what they once were. Apparently it is important that this reminder be given to us repeatedly, following the principle of spaced repetition. "You were once darkness" (v8). Just as the Israelites were never to forget that they were once slaves in Egypt, Christians are never to forget that they were once darkness. The way Paul says this is a bit surprising. We would expect him to say, "You were once in darkness," for this is true. But instead he hits us harder with the fact that we were not just *in* darkness, but we *were* darkness. We were not just trapped in it and imprisoned in it; we had bought into it. Like Patty Hearst (some of you remember her), we were not just kidnapped, but we became terrorists ourselves. We were not just in a problem. We were the problem. We were not just in a mess. We were a mess. Remembering this is important because it guards us from the folly of self-righteousness, as well as from the absurd position of ingratitude.

However, while it is important never to forget who we were, it is even more important to fully grasp who we are — "children of light," "light in the Lord." When I was growing up, there were certain things I would never do because I understood that I was a Jones. There were certain things Joneses did not do. Unfortunately not all the Joneses' guidelines were Biblical. But you get the point. Because of who I understood myself to be, there were certain things I would and would not do. Paul wants us to fully understand who we are, and if we get that on straight, then the behavior that God desires and the actions that God can richly bless will follow.

Some of us hear Paul's statement, and we have doubts. We don't feel much like a child of light. Maybe we feel like a tiny flashlight with a weak battery. Maybe we feel more like a smoldering wick that is just about to go out. We need to see ourselves the way God sees us in Christ. Don't dare to look in that mirror without your faith glasses on. We *are* children of light. We *are* light in the Lord. The light may have become dim, but we follow a Jesus who does not snuff out those dimly burning wicks (Matthew 12:20).

As hard as it may be to believe sometimes, we are the light of the world (Matthew 5:14). Christ has chosen to shine on us and to reflect his perfect light through our imperfect lives. With the power of his Spirit we can be known among our fellows for righteousness, goodness and truth (Ephesians 5:9). It doesn't take money or education or a certain personality to do it either. We must simply have a humble attitude of wanting to "find out what pleases the Lord" (v10). But what a great guiding principle this is. To simply pray in every situation to find out what pleases God and then to be open to the guidance of his word and his people (in that order) will mean that our lives will become a light in a dark world. And here is the amazing thing: The greater our challenges, the brighter our light will shine.

Expose the Darkness

While there is most certainly a positive, uplifting aspect of light, there is also another important aspect: It exposes the darkness and reveals it for what it really is. In our culture so many things are accepted, and fewer and fewer are the people who see a problem with them. I am sitting at my computer as I write this. It is late. My wife is in bed in the next room. With three or four clicks of the mouse at my right hand, I could be on the Internet viewing pornography, and from what I have read and from what I have learned from the people I have counseled, I know there would be volumes of it available to me. National magazines are reporting that far more money is made on the Internet from the sex business than from any other enterprise. Many of your children will come home tomorrow afternoon, turn on MTV, and see what is designed explicitly to promote one thing: lust. The darkness has become accepted in our culture and easily available in our homes — and this is just one area. Add to that the attitudes about abortion, sex outside of marriage, divorce, lying, cheating, greed, partying — and the like. People don't feel that they are so bad because they judge themselves by themselves. They look around and see some extreme cases of evil and feel better about themselves.

But those who "find out what pleases the Lord" will first walk the walk and then talk the talk. They will have something to say. Like Jesus whom they follow, they will love people, but they will challenge them and call them to leave their lives of sin (John 8:11).

People do not respond well to those who expose their sin for them (John 3:20). But this is the moment of truth. Here we find out if we have come into the light because we just want life to go better for us or because we genuinely have the desire to "find out what pleases the Lord." As instruments of his peace, we will find ourselves to be targets in a great spiritual war. It is a righteous battle worth fighting, and we need to hear those fellow believers around us singing:

> "Wake up, O sleeper,
>   rise from the dead,
> and Christ will shine on you."

Taking Inventory

1. In what ways can you say that at one time you "were darkness"?

2. List specific ways that you can be "light in the Lord" in three different situations in your life.

3. What do you fear most about exposing the darkness? Why is it important to let Christ shine on you?

23 The Lord's Will, Not Ours

> Be very careful, then, how you live—not as unwise but as wise, ¹⁶making the most of every opportunity, because the days are evil. ¹⁷Therefore do not be foolish, but understand what the Lord's will is.
>
> Ephesians 5:15-17

"Find out what pleases the Lord," Paul told us in Ephesians 5:10. Every disciple who would live with a pure heart must embrace that simple goal. Having your body in all the right places and going through all the right acts of spirituality counts for nothing unless in your heart is a simple desire to find out one thing: what pleases the Lord. A famous philosopher from the nineteenth century wrote a book titled, *Purity of Heart Is to Will One Thing*. At least the title was right on target. The one thing a disciple wills is to find out what pleases the Lord. We must not be led by our selfish desires, by our need to protect ourselves or by our interest in avoiding pain and finding what is comfortable. We must be led by our desire to find out what pleases the Lord and be committed to that, whatever price it involves.

Understand What the Lord's Will Is

I remember when our three daughters were going through the teen years and wanting to engage in some popular activities in our culture that my wife and I felt were questionable. Sometimes they would say, "But, Dad, the Browns (not their real name) are disciples and they let their children do this." My response was to try to help them understand that we were not following the Browns. Instead we were trying to find out what pleases the Lord. I would tell the girls that we couldn't be sure that we always made exactly the right decisions about such things. I am sure we missed the mark to the left sometimes and to the right at other times. However, I told them I was confident that my guiding principle was the right one. In any situation you will not go far wrong if you study, pray and seek advice with one desire: to "find out what pleases the Lord."

This attitude of heart described in verse 10 is so important that Paul comes back to it with slightly different words in verse 17. Here the principle is expressed as "understand what the Lord's will is." Sometimes such understanding will be simple, obvious and as plain as the nose on your face. Sexual immorality is clearly not the Lord's will (Ephesians 5:3). Stealing and lying are clearly not the Lord's will (Ephesians 4:25, 28). Speaking words that build our brothers or sisters up, just as definitely *is* the Lord's will (4:29). There is no law against love, joy, peace, patience, kindness, goodness and self-control. God wills as much of those as we can get (Galatians 5:22-23).

But at other times more work is required to determine God's will and to surrender our own. Again we are on firm ground when we check our hearts and make sure that what we really want is to understand the Lord's will—even if it turns out to be quite different from what we want. I always know I am on shaky ground whenever I don't want to think things through or I resist praying, "Nevertheless, Lord, not my will, but yours be done." Our hearts are pure only when they will one thing: doing God's will whatever it takes.

Because the Days Are Evil

If we are anything less than firmly resolved to find and do God's will, the forces around us will take over and push us in wrong directions. "Be very careful," Paul writes,

"...because the days are evil" (vv15-16). The person who wants to please the Lord must start with a healthy dose of reality and cannot afford to be naive. This is not a godly world. The attitudes we will get from neighbors, from television, from movies, from literature and from the media will not be godly. We will find some things here and there that are not bad and even a few things that are good, but we must be realistic about the overall environment we live in. The emphasis of our world is not on finding out what pleases the Lord. Its goal is not to show honor and respect to the God who loves us and has made great plans for us. The underlying principle of our society is opposed to following the example of Jesus and laying down our lives for others. Too many disciples forget this and are slowly, but all too surely, accepting ways of thinking that are more from the world than from the Word.

We must not be foolish. We must live as wise, not as unwise. I am reminded of Jesus' statement in Matthew 10:16 when he told the disciples that he was sending them out among wolves and that they must be "wise as serpents, and harmless as doves" (KJV). Very clearly he was saying, "Don't be naive," just as Paul is saying here, "Do not be foolish." It is not a good world out there. People are not trying to please God, and we must be careful that we do not let the world pour us into its mold (Romans 12:2 PHILLIPS). Sure, we have to live in the world and work in the world, but we must not buy into the world's values, attitudes or reactions.

The days are evil; we must never think otherwise. They were evil when Paul wrote this. They were evil in the "good old" simpler times of mid-twentieth century America. They will always be evil. You will never find heaven's values embraced by this world. We will always be strangers and aliens (1 Peter 1:1) — get used to it!

But Paul is not one to just curse the darkness. Notice a phrase in the midst of this discussion: "making the most of every opportunity" (v16). Disciples who are "wise as serpents" and not foolishly sucked into the world's thinking have an incredible opportunity to do exactly what Jesus did — "to seek and to save what was lost" (Luke 19:10). Jesus was able to make the difference he made only because he saw clearly how lost the world was. When we recognize how messed up the world is, when we refuse to follow its principles, when we set our hearts on finding out what the Lord's will is, we have opportunities at every turn to make a difference in people's lives. You are not just another person living next door to someone, another coworker in an office, another student in a classroom. You are not just another shopper in the checkout line. You are a child of light, and you have an opportunity to help someone who is in darkness to find the light. For you, there are opportunities everywhere you turn.

Keep your life simple. Just get up every day with one goal — to find out what pleases the Lord. Struggle, pray, surrender. But make it your one overriding goal to understand what the Lord's will is and to do it. That's being a disciple.

Taking Inventory

1. How do you honestly feel about making it your goal to find out what pleases the Lord so that you can do it?

2. What in God's will do you most struggle with? Write down what you believe a demon from hell might say to you in this struggle and then what you believe an angel from God might say.

3. After looking at what you have written, where is your heart?

4. Why is it liberating to make it your one goal in life to understand what the Lord's will is and to find out what pleases the Lord?

24 Fullness of the Spirit

Do not get drunk on wine, which leads to debauchery. Instead, be filled with the Spirit. [19]Speak to one another with psalms, hymns and spiritual songs. Sing and make music in your heart to the Lord, [20]always giving thanks to God the Father for everything, in the name of our Lord Jesus Christ.

Ephesians 5:18-20

Everybody, it seems, tries to be filled up with something in an effort to deal with life's difficulties. In recent years the church has learned a great deal about how many of us, even in the body of Christ, have used drugs and alcohol to medicate our pain. We have learned that the person with a chemical dependency might be sitting right beside you or even leading your group. Some of us have learned, to our surprise, that we ourselves were that person. Fifteen years ago I would have been among many who never would have believed that such a thing could happen in the church, but we have been given a hard dose of reality. I praise God that we are responding openly, humbly and righteously to what we have been shown. In this passage, Paul warns about sinful and unhealthy ways of coping with life. Medicating with alcohol or drugs is never a solution, but only a temporary fix that leads to serious problems. Instead of using the world's method, he calls us to be filled with the only thing that really meets our need.

Keep on Being Filled

"Be filled with the Spirit." It is such a simple phrase, but a closer examination reveals something very rich and important. Let's take a moment and conjugate this Greek verb *pleroo*. (It turns out there really was something useful about those grammar classes I once found so boring.)

First, we need to notice that this verb is in *the imperative mood*. This means it is a command. The fullness of God's Spirit is not an option for us. We can no more please the Lord without the Spirit of God in our lives than we can drive to work today without gas in our cars. Being filled with the Spirit is something essential and something about which we must be urgent. We will be filled with the Spirit or we will not belong to Christ. (See also Romans 8:9.)

Second, we need to notice that this verb is in *the plural form*, which means this is something for the whole church. Every child of God is to be filled with the Spirit. This is not just for leaders, but for every disciple. But there is more. Already in Ephesians we have seen the connection between the Holy Spirit and the body of Christ. The temple of the Holy Spirit is not just individual Christians in isolation from each other; rather, the temple of the Spirit is the body of Christ. We will not be filled with the Spirit if we are disconnected from one another. Being filled with the Spirit is something that happens to us together with our brothers and sisters. Sure, we all need times alone with God, and yes, those times can be spiritually filling, but we will not maintain what we have found without fellowship. The verb is plural.

Third, we need to notice that this verb is in *the passive voice*. The sentence does not read, "Fill yourself with the Spirit," but "Be filled with the Spirit." We cannot work hard enough to make this happen, but here is what we can do: we can be open and receptive, and we can allow Christ to fill us with the Spirit. We can admit our need and come before him in humility, asking him to put in us what we cannot find on our own. Some of us try to psyche ourselves up. We talk ourselves into taking action. This may work for a while and fool a few people here and there, but it is not the same as humbly opening our lives and allowing God to fill us with his Spirit.

Finally, we must note that this exhortation is in *the present tense*. Had Paul wanted to communicate that this filling of the Holy Spirit was something that happens only once at a definite point in time, he could have used the aorist tense in Greek. But he chose the present tense, which in a context like this one carries with it the idea of *continuous action*. In other words he is saying, "Keep on being filled with the Spirit" or "Be filled with the Spirit again and again." Certainly we were all given the gift of the Spirit at our baptism (Acts 2:38) and that only happens once, but again and again we must let the Spirit fill us with his fruit, his conviction and his renewing power. The days are evil and the world has a way of wearing us all down. Again and again, we must come back to God and his people and allow ourselves to be filled with the Spirit.

There is one last thing to say about this verb, and you don't have to know grammar to see this one. The word "filled" speaks for itself. Paul is calling for us to let the Spirit permeate every area of our lives. Being filled doesn't mean being somewhat filled or partially filled. It means just what it looks like it means—filled!

We are not to be filled with frustration, bitterness or despair; nor are we to be filled with something like alcohol that is designed to cover these things up. We are to be filled completely with the Spirit, who is truly able to deal with life's challenges and bring healing to our minds and hearts.

Making Music

"Out of the overflow of the heart the mouth speaks" (Matthew 12:34). When we are filled with the Spirit, when we are finding real answers to life's challenges, when we experience a deep sense of purpose, when we have the fruit in our lives that causes relationships to be healed, the result will always be music. Thankful and happy people love to sing. They love to express to God and to each other in song those things that have filled their hearts.

But singing not only comes from those who have been filled with the Spirit, it helps the church *to be filled* with the Spirit. Thus, we are told to speak to one another in song. We can lift each other up as we sing. We can encourage each other. We can inspire each other. We must never allow ourselves to come into the assembly, take our songbooks and mumble through the words or songs. When we sing, we must express our hearts to God, focus on building each other up and be open to being filled with the Spirit in fresh ways. Those times when we sing to each other are just as important as those times when someone preaches the Word, but many of us have not believed that. In fact, there are times when music can move our hearts like nothing else can. Without question, Paul sees a connection between the filling of the Spirit and the music of disciples.

Whether we are singing or just living, we are called to "always [give] thanks to God the Father for everything, in the name of our Lord Jesus Christ" (v20). Some of us don't think that this is possible. But here is what I am learning: There is something so powerful about the Spirit that his filling really does enable us to be thankful in *all* circumstances. The filling of the Spirit opens the eyes of our hearts and enables us to see just how much we have been given (do you remember Ephesians 1:18?). There may be plenty of negative things that we could focus on, but the Spirit will help us see that what we have in Christ is so much greater than those challenges. The Spirit will help us to always be giving thanks.

Taking Inventory

1. Are you trying to fill your life up with anything that is not of God? Who will you talk with about that today?

2. What in your life indicates you are serious about being filled with the Spirit?

3. What have you found most enables you to be filled with the Spirit?

4. Why do you want to sing?

25 The Power of Submission

> Submit to one another out of reverence for Christ.
>
> Ephesians 5:21

The heart of the New Testament is the message of the cross. The central tenet of the New Testament is that if we want to find our lives, we must lose them, and if we want to be exalted, we must humble ourselves. When we hear this, we know right away that this book is not normal and does not reflect the wisdom we receive from the world. It should not surprise us then that the Biblical message about how to succeed in relationships is going to fly in the face of conventional wisdom.

In this section of Ephesians, Paul begins with a word that is very nearly despised in our world: *submit*. It is a word universally hated by teenagers, college students, employees and citizens. We can react to this passage and argue that Paul was merely molded by his own culture, or we can humbly come to this text with a desire to learn the deeper spiritual truth that we need.

Submission Is for All of Us

There is room for some difference of opinion as to what this verse introduces (see Mike Van Auken's notes on this chapter in the back of the book). However, when seen in context, verse 21 clearly teaches that submitting to one another is to flow from the filling of the Spirit (Ephesians 5:18). This means it is to be a part of the Christian's lifestyle. Paul has written most of this letter to emphasize that in Christ we have been brought together as one body and one family. The admonition to submit to one another is the logical conclusion to everything he has written about our relationships. We are not to resist one another or pull away from one another or dispute about our rights with one another. We are to submit our lives to one another. Our mentality must not be "How can I get people to do what I want?" but rather, "How can I serve and help and support people so they can be encouraged to become more Christlike?" The world tells you to figure out how people can help you and get them to do it. Jesus tells you to see how you can give to people and make them feel loved, respected, needed and valuable.

The verb used here (hupotasso) normally refers to submission in specifically ordered relationships (e.g., leaders/followers, husbands/wives, parents/children). Our first application of submission must be in those relationships. However, we need to see that having the character of Christ means that there is a way in which submission must flow both ways in every Christian relationship.[1] We should all submit to those who are over us in the Lord (1 Thessalonians 5:12, Hebrews 13:17), which means that we should obey them and support them. In another way, those who lead must learn to submit their lives to their followers, serving them and setting an example for them, and never lording it over them (1 Peter 5:1-4). Submission is not only for all of us; in some sense it is for all of us *in every relationship*.

Jesus' disciples were called to submit to him, but it was not a one-way street. He submitted himself to them and for them. As an elder, I may look at a younger brother who is behaving pridefully and decide that I need to teach him to be humble — and I do. If he wants to grow, he will submit to my correction (1 Peter 5:5). However, I can never do this righteously without seeing that I need to, in another sense, submit myself to him and for him. It is my role to submit to him my time, my energy,

[1] For more study on this, see 1 Peter 2:11-3:8.

my love and my heart. This is the character the first disciples saw in Jesus, and this is what people must see in me.

Submission is of God and it is powerful. The world so often calls good evil and evil good, thus resisting the very thing that causes our relationships to be revived and renewed. If we are having trouble with a relationship, the first thing we need to do is pray for the wisdom to know how to submit to that person. This is the last thing most of us think is needed, but it is what will turn the tide.

God has defined his order in many relationships, including those described at the end of Ephesians 5 and beginning of Ephesians 6. Submission has the primary meaning of obeying and supporting the ones God has placed over us. However, in many situations submission will mean confessing, forgiving, serving or sometimes just listening carefully. It will mean giving of ourselves to others.

In all cases submission means abandoning our pride and putting the other person's good above our own. It means laying down our lives for someone. This is the kind of submission that we see in Jesus. We can be submissive to someone while correcting, or even rebuking him, if we are speaking the truth with love and we are willing to hang in there with him until he changes. If we drop a bomb of truth on someone and leave him to bind up his own wounds and pick up the pieces while we trot on with our lives, we have missed the point.

The Call to the Cross

Submission is so otherworldly, so contrary to the natural man, that even many Christians have never discovered its power and chafe when they hear the word. The call to submission is the call to the cross. We fear submission like we fear the cross, but in both we find the wisdom and power of God. Many of us need to completely change our minds about submission. We must not just reluctantly accept it, but thankfully embrace it.

If submission to one another were not powerful, God would not ask us to do it. Everything he calls us to is designed to draw us closer to him, build greater unity, advance the gospel and help more people to change their lives. The more we submit to one another out of our reverence for Christ, the healthier the church will become; and the healthier it becomes, the more it will grow.

Most of us resist submission in some way. It can be argued that our flesh resists it every day. This is why Jesus said that discipleship involves taking up the cross daily. As we consistently crucify our desire to do things our way, as we consider others better than ourselves (Philippians 2:3), as we look for ways to lay down our lives for each other (1 John 3:16), we will be the children of light Paul has earlier described.

Taking Inventory

1. What is your initial, honest reaction to the idea of submission?

2. In what sense would you say Jesus submitted to us?

3. Why is it helpful to remember that submission to one another is "out of reverence for Christ"?

4. List three different types of relationships you have in which you need to practice submission. Be specific about what you need to do.

26 Marriage in the Plan

Wives, submit to your husbands as to the Lord. [23]For the husband is the head of the wife as Christ is the head of the church, his body, of which he is the Savior. [24]Now as the church submits to Christ, so also wives should submit to their husbands in everything.

[25]Husbands, love your wives, just as Christ loved the church and gave himself up for her [26]to make her holy, cleansing her by the washing with water through the word, [27]and to present her to himself as a radiant church, without stain or wrinkle or any other blemish, but holy and blameless. [28]In this same way, husbands ought to love their wives as their own bodies. He who loves his wife loves himself. [29]After all, no one ever hated his own body, but he feeds and cares for it, just as Christ does the church—[30]for we are members of his body. [31]"For this reason a man will leave his father and mother and be united to his wife, and the two will become one flesh." [32]This is a profound mystery—but I am talking about Christ and the church. [33]However, each one of you also must love his wife as he loves himself, and the wife must respect her husband.

Ephesians 5:22-33

One would be hard pressed to find any institution in our modern culture that has been more assaulted than marriage. For at least the last thirty years, divorce has been viewed as an acceptable option. An increasing number of people today postpone marriage because they have seen so few successes and have so many doubts about how it will work. Of course, it would be a big mistake to think that difficulties in marriages began in the last half century. Sure, most marriages stayed together before the '70s, but one has to question how much quality, fulfillment and intimacy were found in those relationships.

Looking back through the centuries, we find—even in the Bible—only a few marriages that can be held up as exemplary. The history of the human race is not the history of satisfying marriages. It is quite sad that something so well designed by God and something that works so well when handled in a godly way, has been the source of so much pain and frustration. But in spite of man's failures, marriage has a prominent place in God's great plan, and Paul shows us how to find the richness God intended in the marriage relationship.

Wives Who Are Submissive

Paul first calls on wives to be submissive to their husbands. If you have for some reason turned to this chapter without reading the one just before it, you could possibly miss the point. When Paul speaks here of the submission needed by wives, it is most important to understand that this is in the context of a Christian community where everyone is to be submissive in some form to everyone else. When a large religious denomination recently reaffirmed its belief in this passage, a firestorm of protest erupted with many claiming that women were being demeaned and the clock of progress was being turned back. Those who feel that way do not understand the broader New Testament teaching on submission.

Paul describes God's order for the marriage relationship. It is God's plan that the husband be the leader and for the wife to submit to or be subject to that leadership. In our modern culture this is a hard teaching. However, before we react we must understand what this is not saying. This passage does not teach that the wife is to be a silent partner. Submission does not equal silence. It certainly does not mean for the husband to be a domineering force in the marriage or that the wife is to be walked on, as is made clear by the next verses specifically addressed to the men. What this does mean is that the wife must recognize the husband's role and should encourage and support her husband's leadership. When a woman refuses to offer that support and does not submit to her husband, she shows more confidence in her plan than in God's plan. She gives in to pride or, in many cases, to fear (1 Peter 3:5-6).[1]

Submission will not be easy, particularly in our culture. We all have to wrestle with it and figure it out in our own circumstances. It requires much advice and counsel. It humbles us all and drives us to prayer. Remember that it is related to the cross. But as such, it yields good fruit. No one will improve on God's plan. No woman will ever find another path that will help her husband become God's man or her children have a healthier environment in which to grow. As in everything else in the Christian life, we find our lives by losing them.

Husbands Who Love Abundantly

When Paul turns to the husbands, he delivers what may be viewed as an even more challenging admonition. He takes us straight to the cross and calls us to love our wives in the same sacrificial way that Christ loved the church. This is hardly the picture of a man who bosses his wife around and reminds her of her need to submit. Neither is it the picture of a man who comes home from work and crawls into "his cave" and leaves the primary leadership of the family to his wife. No, Paul's words humble all of us who are husbands, bring us to our knees, and cause us to go to God, as did Jesus, to find the strength to get involved and lay down our lives for others.

Coming as they do from a first century Jew and former Pharisee, these words are remarkable. Paul surely grew up

[1] For more help in understanding the role that submission plays in a wife's relationship with her husband, see chapter 3 of *Raising Awesome Kids in Troubled Times* by Sam and Geri Laing (Woburn, Mass.: DPI, 1994) and chapter 4 of *Friends and Lovers* by Sam and Geri Laing (Woburn, Mass.: DPI, 1996).

hearing his mentors thank God they were not born a Gentile or a woman. He probably prayed that prayer himself. He was surrounded by a culture that saw women as primarily existing to serve men. In this passage, he shows he is not just another man who had been molded by such a worldview. Having been transformed in Christ, Paul now calls every Christian husband to love his wife sacrificially and abundantly, making her feel special, treasured and radiant.[2]

Men and Women Who Are Transformed

Our culture most likely has taught us all the wrong lessons. We may have had parents, relatives and friends who set all the wrong examples for us. But in Christ, we can be transformed. Women can trust God enough and love their husbands enough to support them in their leadership. Husbands can be inspired by Jesus to show their wives the greatest consideration, and do it unconditionally. Wives and husbands who try but fail each other (as all of us will from time to time) can together return to the cross to forgive and be forgiven. With each passing year they can discover more about how perfectly God's great plan for marriage fits with his great plan for our redemption. What the world has so much trouble figuring out, we can discover again and again at the foot of the cross.

---

[2] For more help in understanding how a husband leads his wife in a godly way, see chapter 3 of *Friends and Lovers* by Sam and Geri Laing (Woburn, Mass.: DPI, 1996).

Taking Inventory

1. Wives, carefully read the part written to you in Ephesians 5. Husbands, carefully read the part written to you. What does it say about you when you would rather read *to your spouse* the part that was intended for him or her?

2. If you are married, write down two changes that you want to make because of this text and share these with your spouse.

3. If you are unmarried, what attitudes does this passage teach you to have in other relationships? If you marry in the future, what do you think will be the most challenging part of your God-designed role?

4. A special challenge for husbands and wives: Read the part of this text that is addressed to you once a week for the next year. Each time you read, pray that you will go to the cross for your spouse.

27 Families in the Plan

Children, obey your parents in the Lord, for this is right. [2]"Honor your father and mother"— which is the first commandment with a promise— [3]"that it may go well with you and that you may enjoy long life on the earth."

[4]Fathers, do not exasperate your children; instead, bring them up in the training and instruction of the Lord.

Ephesians 6:1-4

Children actually obeying parents? Talk about a strange idea, at least to those who live in the modern Western world. Go in any grocery store or department store today and watch the interaction between children and parents. Who's calling the shots? Most of the time it is Johnny or Suzie. Mom says, "Johnny come over here." He either ignores her and does his own thing or rudely says, "No, I want to go over there." Dad picks Suzie up at her friend's and says, "It's time to go." Often the response is "No, I don't want to go. I want to stay longer." Parents seem intimidated and lost.

Check out Hollywood's latest depiction of family life. Who is portrayed as being more with it and more cool and more intelligent? Today's screen versions of Mom and Dad are bumbling, frustrated people who have little if any control over their more clever, witty and often foul-mouthed children. This was never God's plan and it must not be what happens in our homes today.

Honor Your Father and Mother

As we saw earlier, our goal in life must be to find out what pleases the Lord, to find out what God's good, pleasing and perfect will is. When it comes to children, there is no doubt what God's will is. It is stated very early in the Bible: "Honor your father and your mother." Every child, in a word, is to be humble in his relationship with his mother and father. He is to show honor and respect to them simply because they are his parents. Until that child leaves his father and mother to live his own adult life, he is to obey them. Even then, the principle of honoring them is to be maintained.

There are two ways most of us need to apply this important principle. First, we must look at our relationships with our parents. If we were disobedient to them when we lived under their supervision or if we treat them now with anything less than honor, we need to repent and ask for forgiveness. Do our parents feel we respect them? Do they feel we value them? Do they feel we are humble in our relationship with them? If we cannot answer yes to all those questions, we probably have to make some changes. To paraphrase something the apostle John said, if we do not show respect to our parents on earth whom we have seen, how can we show respect to God, the Father, whom we have not seen?

Second, if we have children, we must not let the world win the day. All around us and all around them will be examples of disobedient children who treat their parents with contempt. We must not lower the bar. God's standard is for children to obey and to honor. We are not asking too much when we expect our children to do exactly what God has said.

I find entirely too many parents in the church who allow their children to be disrespectful without consequences. They are making a serious mistake that will produce some bad fruit. It takes courage, prayer and advice to win some of these battles, but if we love our children, these battles must be won.

Bring Them Up

When Paul gives us basic parenting principles, he does not specifically address mothers here, but instead speaks to fathers. Let me say two things about this. First, the Bible is very clear that fathers are to be the spiritual leaders in the home. This is not so much a position of privilege but of responsibility. Too many men leave the spiritual training and the disciplining of their children to their wives. Too many men find they aren't naturally good at leading family devotionals, so they don't do it. They withdraw and do only what they feel they can do successfully. This is "disorderly conduct"—conduct that brings disorder into a family. No one will arrest you for it, but when all is said and done, there will be high price to pay. Children need to see Dad honoring God, being open about his faith, courageously calling his family to live by God's standards, and taking the lead in the tough task of disciplining. No dad will do it perfectly (and we all need to be open about our failures), but every child needs a dad who is earnest about the spiritual life.

The second thing I want to say is that there is a principle here for mothers and fathers. We are to teach our children to respect age and authority, but we are also to treat them with respect. Paul says, "Do not exasperate your children." The Greek word *parogizo* means to provoke to anger. This is something we can do in a variety of ways. We can have one standard for ourselves and a different standard for our children. In other words, we can be hypocrites. We can make promises and not deliver. We can ignore our children's need for focused attention. We can tolerate their disobedience until we finally reach a point of explosion. We can ridicule or demean their efforts. We can smother them with too many rules and demands. In my case, I was guilty of being sarcastic and had to be corrected. This is not a complete list. There are other ways we can treat our children disrespectfully and frustrate them. Paul is basically telling us to apply the golden rule with our children and treat them the way we want to be treated.

Once we are loving them and treating them as valuable, then we can bring them up in the training and instruction of the Lord. In other words, we can lead them down the path we ourselves have chosen to go. The words for "training" and "instruction" (*paideia* and *nouthesia*) both imply the need for correction. Any child left to go his or her own way will take another road and not find God's plan. God's way has to be learned. Teaching and training are required for all. Such training must never be harsh and must always be full of grace. It must involve humility and confession on the part of those who administer it imperfectly. But it must never be compromised. The stakes are just too high.

Family life is a foretaste of heaven, but only when we do it God's way.

Taking Inventory

1. Have you fully repented of your own disrespectful attitudes toward your parents? Have they heard your confession and request for forgiveness?

2. This week, this month, this year, what can you do to honor your mother and father?

3. Parents, if someone spent a week in your home, would they find children who respect their parents and understand that it is God's will for them to honor you? If not, whom will you ask for help?

4. Parents, how do you exasperate your children? Why is it so essential that you make changes?

28 The Workplace in the Plan

Slaves, obey your earthly masters with respect and fear, and with sincerity of heart, just as you would obey Christ. ⁶Obey them not only to win their favor when their eye is on you, but like slaves of Christ, doing the will of God from your heart. ⁷Serve wholeheartedly, as if you were serving the Lord, not men, ⁸because you know that the Lord will reward everyone for whatever good he does, whether he is slave or free.

⁹And masters, treat your slaves in the same way. Do not threaten them, since you know that he who is both their Master and yours is in heaven, and there is no favoritism with him.

Ephesians 6:5-9

Many have questioned why the New Testament does not advocate the overthrow of slavery. As we have already seen, Paul and others like him, and most certainly Jesus, were not timid about challenging ungodly cultural norms. We can only speculate as to why the almost universal practice of slavery was never condemned, but this much we can say: the application of the Christian ethic would have removed *every* abuse associated with slavery and eventually did lead to its rejection. Paul's letter to Philemon shows that the master-slave relationship had to be viewed in a completely different way in Christ. Paul's ultimate goal was that Philemon would view Onesimus "no longer as a slave, but better than a slave, as a dear brother" (v16).

Paul's instructions to slaves here, in 1 Corinthians and in Colossians, along with Peter's words in 1 Peter, are important for us today, even though slavery is now illegal around the world. While none of us are slaves, we do all have relationships with superiors who are responsible for overseeing our work. If the principles described here were right for Christians who had a slave-master relationship, they are certainly applicable to us who enjoy more freedom and opportunity.

When Another Is over You

Slaves who were Christians were to be obedient to those who were over them. They were to obey as if they were obeying Christ. They were not to just obey and work hard when they were under the watchful eye of a supervisor, but they were to serve as if serving Christ whose eye is never closed to what they—and we—are doing. Even though their working conditions were far from ideal, they were to serve wholeheartedly, focusing on the fact they were really serving Christ and not just men. Even if their earthly supervisors did not show appreciation for their hard work, they could be sure that the Lord was not missing anything and that he would reward them richly for what they were doing.

Paul is saying that as Christians we are to view our vocations entirely differently. We are not simply helping men to accomplish their goals, but we are being given an opportunity to show Christ to the world through the way we work. What stands out to me is that we are called to go to the cross, even when our circumstances are the most challenging. Christian slaves were to die to their sense of injustice or to their right to be resentful. They were to crucify any bitterness about their treatment. Paul tells slaves in the Corinthian church that it is fine to try to win their freedom, but if it does not work out, they must live Jesus' lifestyle right where they are and be grateful that in Christ they have ultimate freedom (1 Corinthians 7:21-24). This is a hard teaching for some of us, but it shows that the call to deny ourselves and take up the cross is a call that knows no exceptions.

Yes, being disrespected or disregarded hurts us. Yes, such painful feelings have to be processed and talked through; they cannot just be stuffed. But at the end of the day, the disciple must end up back at the cross where he will discover again that what the world so despises really *is* the wisdom and power of God. What we sometimes cling to so tightly — our right to be recognized, respected and honored by men — is just a fleeting thing. It is far greater to do what is pleasing in the eyes of God. In her book *9 to 5 and Spiritually Alive*, my wife, Sheila, wrote these words:

> It doesn't matter what we do — sell cars, type reports, clean houses, teach classes, give shots, write books, answer phones, conduct hearings, give performances, moderate debates, execute wills, do surgery — we should give our best. We owe it to our clients/customers, our employers, our employees, our coworkers, ourselves and our God. When we hold back from giving our best, we are robbing our employers, and we are robbing God.[1]

For today's disciples this is the message of Ephesians: follow directions, be a team player, work wholeheartedly, and do it all joyfully because you belong to Christ and have an opportunity to shine for him.

When You Are over Others

Those who were masters in the ancient world had unlimited rights to do whatever they wanted to do to their slaves since the slave was the master's property. But once a master became a Christian, he was to love his neighbor, and his slave was his neighbor. Once a master followed Jesus, he was to treat each person, slave or free, the way Jesus would treat that person. Just as the Christian slave was to serve as if serving Christ, so the Christian master was to treat those under him with the consciousness that he himself was living under the authority of Christ. Suddenly the whole dynamic between master and slave was changed.

[1] Sheila Jones, *9 to 5 and Spiritually Alive* (Woburn, Mass.: DPI, 1997), 79.

When Paul says, "Do not threaten them," the phase in Greek carries with it the idea of no longer threatening. What is implied is that this was the normal way of relating to slaves. Since they were not, in most cases, highly motivated to serve out of love, most masters felt that slaves had to be compelled to serve out of fear. Once becoming a Christian, a master was to create an environment entirely free from intimidation. He was to motivate in an entirely different way. Was this difficult? We can be sure it was. But the master had to learn to stand humbly with his slaves under the Master who is in heaven.

Today, we live a different world. None of us, thank God, have slaves, but many of us are responsible for supervising the work of others. We have the authority to direct them, to discipline them and to fire them if necessary. Such authority must be employed in all humility. We must realize that we are accountable to God for our treatment of others. We must fulfill our own duty, see that the tasks assigned our team are fulfilled and work hard to reach goals, but we must care for people, even as God has cared for us. We should follow one simple rule: Treat others as we ourselves would want to be treated.

Taking Inventory

1. Try to imagine being a first century slave who became a Christian. What would be your greatest challenge?

2. Why do you think the New Testament is not sentimental about slaves and does not make excuses for anger or bitterness that they might feel?

3. What principles are here that you need to apply in your current work situation?

4. For those of you who supervise others, what are three principles you will use to guide all your interactions with those you oversee?

29 Victory in the Plan

Finally, be strong in the Lord and in his mighty power. [11]Put on the full armor of God so that you can take your stand against the devil's schemes. [12]For our struggle is not against flesh and blood, but against the rulers, against the authorities, against the powers of this dark world and against the spiritual forces of evil in the heavenly realms. [13]Therefore put on the full armor of God, so that when the day of evil comes, you may be able to stand your ground, and after you have done everything, to stand. [14]Stand firm then, with the belt of truth buckled around your waist, with the breastplate of righteousness in place, [15]and with your feet fitted with the readiness that comes from the gospel of peace. [16]In addition to all this, take up the shield of faith, with which you can extinguish all the flaming arrows of the evil one. [17]Take the helmet of salvation and the sword of the Spirit, which is the word of God. [18]And pray in the Spirit on all occasions with all kinds of prayers and requests. With this in mind, be alert and always keep on praying for all the saints.

Ephesians 6:10-18

"Life is difficult." So begins a book that has been a best-seller for the last twenty years. This simple line connected with millions of readers. Every person finds life to be such. But once you have signed on to be a disciple of Jesus, there are some unique difficulties that will come your way. Normal life is full of challenges, but the man or woman who steps out of the crowd, embraces God's great plan, and identifies himself or herself with Jesus Christ will especially be under attack. Such a person has declared war on what Paul calls "the spiritual forces of evil in the heavenly realms." Look in the face of a modern terrorist and you will see the same hate that fills the heart of our spiritual enemy. And so, for the believer in Christ, life is a battle. If we are to win (and we certainly can win), we must pay careful attention to what this passage says.

Strength from God, Not Ourselves

Paul puts the most important idea first: "Be strong in the Lord and in his mighty power" (v10). Very quickly he moves on to describe the rulers, principalities, dark powers and evil forces that we are up against. The key is to find our strength in the Lord because no matter how powerful the enemy may be, he and his legions are no match for the Lord of lords and the King of kings. The enemy who opposes us looks unbeatable until we view him beside Almighty God, who made heaven and earth. Like the nations Isaiah described (Isaiah 40:15), the devil and his demons are but a drop in a bucket.

Why does God even allow such an enemy? You can speculate on that if you like. You can work to make sense of it if you please. The Bible just tells that he is real and he is out to destroy us. Then it tells us how we can win against him. If we are in a battle with an intruder, we don't stop to figure out how he entered our house. We concentrate on surviving. We can work on other questions later. In the same way, the Scriptures tell us we are under attack and how to triumph over that attack. For now this is the relevant information.

The key to winning is simple—we must stay close to God. This means staying humble before God, acknowledging how great our need is. Only the poor in spirit inherit the kingdom of heaven (Matthew 5:3). Only in the Lord do we find the "mighty power" that enables us to have a decisive victory over the enemy.

We are all naturally a combination of strengths and weaknesses. The biggest mistake most of us make in the spiritual fight—and it can be a fatal one—is relying on our strengths. We may have intellectual gifts, organization skills or a great sense of humor. The most natural thing in the world is to *rely* on our strengths, to accentuate them, to depend on them, to focus on them. Certainly these can be used by God; but if we rely on these strengths, our clever enemy will employ his schemes (v11) and turn our strengths into weaknesses.

Relying on our own strengths leads to arrogance, pride, competitiveness and humanism. Of course, all of these lead to spiritual defeat. Ironically, what is best (and the forces behind the self-esteem movement will hate this) is for us to focus on our weaknesses, and then let what we see there motivate us to rely on God and not on ourselves. Is this not the lesson God wanted Paul to learn in 2 Corinthians 12? Is it not the reason Paul finally makes the strange statement, "When I am weak, then I am strong"? (2 Corinthians 12:10).

The Armor of God

Many good commentaries help us to understand the different metaphors Paul employs in this passage.[1] We will all profit from a careful examination of each metaphor and an understanding of the analogies that he uses. However, for our purposes here let me ask you to look at the complete list of tools, armor and weapons that he describes and to take some time to meditate on each word or phrase:

- Truth
- Righteousness
- The gospel of peace
- Faith
- Salvation
- The word of God
- Prayer

What strikes you? What do you notice that is not here? What I notice is that none of my strengths is here. What will

---

[1] You can also find more information in the additional notes in the back of this book.

give me victory over the enemy is dependence on God and humility before him.

I will win when I accept his truth, rather than depending on my logic. I will have victory when I accept the righteousness of Christ, rather than trying to establish my own. I will see results when I preach the gospel (and that means the cross), not my words of wisdom. My greatest need is to care for my faith, not my psyche. Remembering that I am saved and that my name is written in heaven will lead me to rejoice and stay in the fight even in challenging times. It is the word of God, not my thinking, that will demolish Satan's stronghold. It is prayer — the humble acknowledgment of weakness and need — that will bring me the resources of Almighty God.

Those of you who are leaders should apply these principles to the building of your ministry. Do you rely on your strengths? Or do you boast in your weaknesses and rely on God's power alone? Very often our efforts to build are frustrated because we foolishly try to build a spiritual house in an unspiritual and worldly way. We pay far too much attention to what brings success in the corporate world, and the enemy laughs. We read too many books on worldly leadership, and we don't spend enough time remembering that "the foolishness of God is wiser than man's wisdom, and the weakness of God is stronger than man's strength" (1 Corinthians 1:25).

Life is difficult. The Christian's life is a battle. But we have a cause. We have a reason to fight. And we can win if we don't fight as the world does.

We must remember the words Moses spoke to Israel: "The Lord will fight for you; you need only to be still" (Exodus 14:14). Let us focus on our weaknesses until we are sure we can win only if we find our strength in the Lord and in his mighty power.

Taking Inventory

1. What are the main elements in the spiritual struggle for you personally?

2. What are the main elements in the struggle for your church?

3. What personal strengths do you tend to rely on when you are in a battle? Once you have identified these, what decision will you make about them?

4. What decisions do you need to make that will ensure that you are relying on God and not on yourself?

5. For leaders: What change do you need to make in the way you lead your ministry?

30 Fearlessly, As I Should

Pray also for me, that whenever I open my mouth, words may be given me so that I will fearlessly make known the mystery of the gospel, [20]for which I am an ambassador in chains. Pray that I may declare it fearlessly, as I should.

[21]Tychicus, the dear brother and faithful servant in the Lord, will tell you everything, so that you also may know how I am and what I am doing. [22]I am sending him to you for this very purpose, that you may know how we are, and that he may encourage you.

[23]Peace to the brothers, and love with faith from God the Father and the Lord Jesus Christ. [24]Grace to all who love our Lord Jesus Christ with an undying love.

Ephesians 6:19-24

God's great plan has been made known to us. By grace, we understand the most important things about life. We have answers. You and I know what our next-door neighbors need to know. You know what the person in the cubicle next to you must learn. You understand something that your doctor or lawyer or bank president has no clue about.

Sure, if you never open your mouth and pass on the gospel to them, most of them will manage to get through life. Most of them will live until retirement. Many will do quite well with their careers and their investments. At the same time, many will have affairs, get divorced, develop strained relationships with their kids. More than a few will become addicted to alcohol, drugs (legal and illegal), pornography or soap operas. Most of them will live into their seventies or eighties and at the end die in a sterile hospital room, with a handful of people then attending a funeral led by someone who hardly knew them. They will have their ups and downs, but most will have lived, laughed, made love, traveled to distant spots, had some fun, made some friends, built something they were proud of, enjoyed skiing down a mountain or riding in an open car or walking on a beach. But then they will die having missed the plan, having never understood why they were here.

Whenever I Open My Mouth

Last night my wife and I spent time with some close friends just marveling at how God's plan has unfolded in our lives. Now, in a few minutes I will go out to pick up some lunch. The young man or woman at the drive-through window whom I will see needs the understanding of God's plan that we have. After picking up lunch, I will cross the street to pick up my laundry. The man who will hand me my shirts needs to know the Jesus I know. I don't know these people, but I know what they need. The friends we are inviting to go with us to a movie tonight need every resource that God can give because their family is out of control—a ship without a rudder. I need to say to all my Christian friends, "Pray for me, that whenever I open my mouth, words will be given me." I have been blessed. "Woe to me if I do not preach the gospel" (1 Corinthians 9:16).

Thanks be to God for those who opened their mouths and shared the message with me. Praise be to God for every person who helped me understand what it means to follow Jesus. Thanks be to God for those books (most of them discovered and read by me after the authors had died) that convinced me that life had a purpose and it was found in Christ. Praise God for every man and woman he so graciously put in my life to help me develop faith in his great plan. Having been given so much, what else can I say but "Pray that I may declare it [the gospel] fearlessly, as I should" to Christian and to non-Christian alike? What else makes sense but for me to care that every disciple I know stands in awe of God, develops deep convictions and lives a life worthy of the calling we have received (Ephesians 4:1), and that every non-Christian comes to understand the commitment God has made to him?

Pray Also for Me

Between now and when you and I die, we will open our mouths many times. But what will come out? Will we speak words that befit people who understand that the Master has a plan, or we will engage mostly in idle chatter that signifies nothing at all and leads no one to the real destination? Paul does the right thing here. He asks those who knew him to pray for him that he would not fail. Most of us are not doing as well in our ambassadorship for Christ as we know we ought to be doing. But the answer is not found in whipping ourselves into action and then relying on ourselves to produce some result. The answer is found in humbling ourselves and asking others to pray for us, so that the strength to act will come from God.

As I write this, I realize I have a unique opportunity. Several thousand of you will likely read this book. I have never had that many people praying for me, but I want to follow Paul's example. I am asking you what Paul asked of the disciples in the province of Asia. Pray also for me, that whenever I open my mouth, words may be given me so that I will fearlessly make known the mystery of the gospel. I am not in chains as he was, but MS has put some definite and ever-growing limits on what I can do. But this has happened that I might not rely on myself but on God, who raises the dead (2 Corinthians 1:9). With your prayers and the help of the Spirit of Jesus Christ, this will turn out for my deliverance. Christ can be exalted in my body, whether by life or by death (Philippians 1:19-20). And who are you asking to pray for you?

When we begin planning for the publishing of a book, one of the first things we do is form a prayer team. They pray for the author and the editors. They pray for the design process. They pray for the printing. Who is on your prayer team? Who have you asked to pray for you that you would declare the message fearlessly, as you should? You don't have to have thousands people praying for you, but you need to demonstrate that you need others praying for you. If Paul needed the prayers of others — and he most certainly did — we are no different.

Faith, Love, Grace and Peace

Our world knows little of peace. As I write this final chapter, the United States is involved in a contentious political debate. The Middle East is a powder keg, as it has been for centuries. Wars rage all over Africa. Racial and ethnic tensions in many places are as high as ever. Homes are full of disrespectful children. Husbands and wives eat dinner each night in tense silence. Neighborhoods look fairly calm, but then you find out what really goes on behind some of the closed doors. We lived for ten years in Concord, Massachusetts, a picturesque town with civic pride and calm streets, but one of Concord's most illustrious citizens described life in his time and in ours when he said, "The mass of men lead lives of quiet desperation."

But the Master has a plan that brings peace. It shows us how to have faith in him, how to accept and love our families and our neighbors, and how to receive and to extend grace to others. All of this leads to peace with God and with others...and peace within ourselves. It is significant that Paul ends this letter with these four great words: faith, love, grace and peace. The Master's plan is that we would all find these in Christ. Once we find them, we must let nothing keep us from proclaiming them to the world. The Master has a plan, and he plans for us to tell it to everyone we know. Let us do so out of our undying love for Jesus Christ.

Taking Inventory

1. Write out why you want to declare the message of Jesus fearlessly to those around you.

2. What is the difference in being fearless and foolish in the way you present the gospel?

3. List the people who you need to ask to be on your prayer team—those who will pray consistently that you will recognize and seize your opportunities.

4. Which word do you most need to focus on—faith, love or grace—in order to see the peace of God? Why?

Additional Notes
Mike Van Auken

Chapter One

Verse 1: The words "in Ephesus" do not appear in some of the earliest manuscripts. This, connected with the fact that the letter is without many personal references, causes some to conclude that it was actually a "circular letter" intended for many churches in Asia Minor, with the name of Ephesus — the principle church in the region — being added later.

Verse 3: The expression "the heavenly realms" appears also in Ephesians 1:20, 2:6, 3:10 and 6:12. It is not a synonym for heaven, but rather, a reference to the spiritual realm. God is there (in the first three references), but the rulers and powers of darkness are also found there (the latter two references). The spiritual battles are ultimately fought in the "heavenly realms," which are not a part of the space/time universe.

The layered conception of the spiritual world probably has its roots in Old Testament and apocryphal Judaism. Various early writers reference five, seven and ten heavens.[1] In 2 Corinthians 12:2, Paul refers to "the third heaven" in a similar fashion.

One key aspect of the multitiered heavens is that the greater beings occupy the higher heavens. Christ's place is obvious: "far above all rule and authority, power and dominion" (Ephesians 1:20-21). Less obvious perhaps is our place as disciples in the heavenly realms. We are seated with Christ (Ephesians 2:6). Therefore, the presence and activity of spiritual enemies in our lives should be of no cause for ultimate concern. Our position, our access to power and our ultimate fate is tied directly to all-powerful Jesus (Matthew 28:18), if we just hold on to him (Hebrews 3:14).

[1] Marty Wooten, *Power in Weakness* (Woburn, Mass.: DPI, 1996), 153-155.

Verse 4: Several commentators believe that in the Greek text the words "in love" attach more naturally to the thoughts that precede them in verse 4 than to the thoughts that follow in verse 5. Note the emphasis on the qualities of our love if the text were to read, "For he chose us in him before the creation of the world to be holy and blameless in his sight in love."

Verse 5: God's predestination does not depend on who the person is specifically, but rather on the individual's response to the cross of Jesus. God's desire, his "pleasure and will," is for "all men to be saved and to come to a knowledge of the truth" (1 Timothy 2:4). He therefore prepared a plan by which all men could be saved through the cross (Hebrews 2:9). God has predestined that all those who respond with obedience to that plan (Hebrews 5:9) will be saved.[2]

Verse 9: God's mystery is obviously a key theme in the book of Ephesians. The Greek word *musterion* carries the idea of a secret that must be—and has now been—revealed in order for us to understand it. It does not mean something that we cannot understand. In other words God is letting us in on his special plan.

Verse 10: The phrase "to bring all things...together" (anakephalaioo) indicates the main point or summary. Paul is emphasizing that Christ is both the instrument (by Christ) and focus (in Christ) in God's plan to unify all things in heaven and on earth. The only other New Testament use of this word is in Romans 13:9 when Paul writes "whatever other commandments there may be, *are summed up* in this one rule: 'Love your neighbor as yourself'" (emphasis mine).

Verse 14: In addition to meaning "earnest money," the word for "deposit" (*arrabon*) is also the root of the modern Greek word for an engagement ring.

Verse 22: There may be times that we feel like the Hebrew writer who wrote:

---

[2] See also Gordon Ferguson's study guide to the book of Romans, *Justified: Just As If I'd Never Sinned* (Woburn, Mass.: DPI, 1992), 29-30 and Douglas Jacoby's treatment of predestination in *Q & A: Answers to Bible Questions You Have Asked* (Woburn, Mass.: DPI, 2001), part 4, question 8.

> In putting everything under him, God left nothing that
> is not subject to him. Yet at present we do not see every-
> thing subject to him. (Hebrews 2:8b)

However, to our God, the subjection of the heavenly realms to Christ is an accomplished fact—for he sees the end from the beginning. Disciples can rejoice since our destiny is linked with his, as the body is to the head. (See also Psalm 8:6.)

Chapter Two

Verses 2-3: The phrases "those who are disobedient" (v2) and "objects of wrath" (v3) translate more literally as "*sons* of disobedience" and "*children* of wrath." Paul's wording is reminiscent of Jesus' language in John 8:39ff. If we choose to live our lives contrary to the plan of God, by default we choose Satan as our father.

Verse 5: Only God can bring the dead to life. Paul sounds much as he does in Romans 5-6 as he talks in this verse about the power of the cross and the role of baptism in our lives. Jesus' physical life, death and resurrection again serve as a model for our spiritual death, burial and resurrection at baptism.

Verse 6: When we are raised with Christ at baptism, we are seated with Christ in "the heavenly realms." This is true no matter how "good" or "bad" today was for us, and it means that we are fully equipped to fight the spiritual battle.

Verse 11: The Greek word *cheiropoietos,* translated "made with hands," is a word used to refer to idols and that which is made by human hands—as opposed to God's. All other New Testament uses of this word refer to man-made temples (Mark 14:58, Acts 7:48, Acts 17:24, Hebrews 9:11, 24).

Verse 12: "Covenants of the promise" may refer to the series of Old Testament messianic covenants given to Abraham (Genesis 17:1-21), Isaac (Genesis 26:2-5), Jacob (Genesis 28:13-15), the nation of Israel (Exodus 24:1-8) and David (2 Samuel 7:11-16), along with the one foundational promise to Abraham

(Genesis 12:1-3). Additional covenants that Paul may have in view include those given to Noah in Genesis 9:8-17 and to Abraham in Genesis 15:7-21.

Verse 13: Isaiah 57:19 says, "Peace, peace, to those far and near," probably referring to God's plan of including the Gentiles in Christ. By the time of the first century, "brought near" was a term used by Jews for Gentile converts to Judaism. The thought was that by drawing near to the Israelite community, that person drew near to God, who was near his people. Here, however, Paul is not talking about including the Gentiles in the "old" Jewish nation, but about including both Jews and Gentiles in an entirely new community.

Verse 14: There are several possibilities as to the meaning of the "dividing wall of hostility." First, Paul mentions the Mosaic Law. Clearly the covenant of circumcision served as a barrier. It was not only a distinguishing mark between Israel and its neighbors, but also a significant deterrent to conversion! Another possibility in the mind of Paul was the physical temple wall between the Court of the Gentiles and the rest of the temple area. Warnings, some of which archaeologists have recovered, were posted on the wall warning any Gentiles who might enter that death was a possible punishment if they were discovered. Ironically, Paul was accused of bringing non-Jews into the temple in Acts 21:27ff.

Verse 15: The Greek word *kainos,* translated "new," shows just how radical Jesus' plan for his church is. It carries the idea of something not previously present — something unknown, strange or remarkable. In his church, Jesus creates an entirely new kind of man. The New Revised Standard Version translates this as "one new humanity."

Verse 18: Our access to God is something very special indeed. The Greek word for "access," *prosagoge,* comes from a verb used to describe introducing a person into the presence of a king.

Verse 20: When Paul writes about the "prophets" here, he is probably referring to New Testament prophets as opposed to both Old and New Testament prophets. First, the word order (apostles listed before prophets) argues against the idea that Paul had Old Testament prophets in mind. Recall 1 Corinthians 12:28, which says, "God has appointed first of all apostles, second prophets...."

Second, Paul uses the same basic construction in two other passages in Ephesians whose contexts can only be taken to mean New Testament prophets: In Ephesians 3:5 he refers to a mystery that has only now been revealed, and in Ephesians 4:11 he discusses church leadership and roles.

Chapter Three

Verse 1: Paul was always aware of his "double address" as a Christian. In the world of course he was a prisoner of Rome. In his heart he was a prisoner of Jesus.

Verse 2: Suddenly Paul digresses. Apparently, as he thinks about the Gentiles to whom he is writing, he starts thinking about the grace of God and many of its implications in his life and in the lives of the letter's recipients. He is compelled to write about them. His example is powerful for us: How overwhelmed with excitement do we get when we consider the grace of God?

Verse 7: The type of servant to which Paul is referring is the *diakonos*. This word is the root of our word "deacon." Note how grateful Paul was for the "gift of God's grace" which enabled him to serve the gospel. In verses 2-8, he uses "grace" three times, "given" three times and "gift" once. All three words come from the same root word in Greek (*charis*).

Verses 10-11: Part of God's role for the church in his eternal plan is coming into view here. We (the church) are God's physical demonstration of his wisdom to both the friendly and hostile spiritual worlds. The word translated as "manifold" (*polupoikilos*) conveys the idea of "multicolored" in Greek. In other words, God's wisdom is not one-dimensional or narrow in any sense — and neither is his church. Of course in the church, God unites Jew and Gentile in Christ. God's plan goes beyond that though, to a unified cosmos (Ephesians 1:9-10). The unity in the church is a key part of the plan and the proof that his plan has already been "accomplished in Christ Jesus our Lord."

Verse 14: With the words "for this reason," Paul returns to the thought that he began in the first verse. Two things in particular stand out as Paul describes his prayer: (1) he is kneeling and (2) he addresses God as "Father." Apparently, standing was a very common posture for prayer for the first century Jew (Mark 11:25, Luke 18:11, 13). To kneel signified great reverence and submission. The address "Father" implies both intimacy and respect. In his letter, Paul uses the term for the One who is the source of grace and peace (Ephesians 1:2) and all good things (Ephesians 5:20). He also uses "Father" for the One deserving of praise (Ephesians 1:3), who is omnipresent (Ephesians 4:6) and into whose presence we come as into the presence of a king (see note on Ephesians 2:18).

Verses 18-19: Paul's prayer is not that we love Christ more, as fitting as that may also be. Paul's prayer is that we would understand and recognize Christ's love for us. He has already described it as "unsearchable" (Ephesians 3:8), so it makes sense that he would call for divine assistance to know and understand it.

Verse 20: God's ability to bless us is beyond comprehension. The King James Version says that he is able to do "exceeding abundantly" more than all we ask. The Greek word translated as "abundantly" (*huperekperissou*) is the "highest form of comparison imaginable."[3] There is no limit to what God can do. Perhaps his power to bless our lives is matched only by his desire to do so.

Verse 21: When Paul writes "to him be glory," he does not wish or hope that God gets the glory, nor does he assign God the glory. Instead, he is simply recognizing a fact: The glory all belongs to God. If Paul, as effective as he was, saw everything he accomplished as being a result of God's grace and power, rather than as accomplished through his own efforts, how much more do we need to assess our own desire for recognition and glory?

---

[3] Walter Bauer, *A Greek-English Lexicon of the New Testament and other Early Christian Literature.* Arndt, Gingrich and Danker, eds. (Chicago: University of Chicago Press, 1979), s.v. *uperekperissou.* (The common abbreviation for this work is BAGD.)

Chapter Four

Verse 2: It took Christianity to make humility a virtue. Prior to Jesus, humility was a character trait to which no one in his right mind would aspire. It was associated with being weak, of low position and servile. The elevation of humility to a godly virtue is just one more example of the wisdom of God being the exact opposite of the wisdom of man.

Gentleness (or meekness) is yet another example of the wisdom of God being greater than the wisdom of man. What Paul's contemporary world (and too often even disciples today!) thought to be a sign of weakness, God ultimately holds up to be a fruit of the Spirit (Galatians 5:23). Gentleness encompasses the idea of power under control or a willingness to waive our rights for the benefit of others. Among other things, it characterizes how we are to treat one another when restoring someone who has sinned and the spirit with which we are to carry each others' burdens (Galatians 6:1-2).

Verse 3: The verb that is translated "make every effort" (*spoudazo*) carries with it the idea of some urgency. It means to hasten or hurry along with diligence and eagerness.

Unity in God's church is a cooperative effort. It is Spirit-made, but man-maintained. The challenge with unity is that while everyone wants to enjoy its fruits, a tremendous amount of effort is required to maintain the type of relationships that Jesus challenges us to have (John 13:34-35, 17:20-23). This is especially true because the "burden of maintenance" falls on the brother or sister who has been hurt. Unity can only be built when we care more about the kingdom of God than about our personal feelings.

Verse 8: The footnote in the New International Version says that Paul is quoting Psalm 68:18 in this verse. However, Psalm 68:18 reads:

> When you ascended on high,
>   you led captives in your train;
>   you received gifts from men...

— rather than (as Paul wrote):

> When he ascended on high,
> he led captives in his train;
> and gave gifts to men.

The question is: Did Paul misquote Psalm 68, or is there another explanation? It certainly seems unlikely that someone with Paul's extensive rabbinical training would misquote it accidentally. There are at least two other perspectives that merit consideration.

First, Paul could have been working with a different Old Testament textual tradition than that with which we are most familiar. The Syriac Peshitta and the Aramaic Targum (early translations of Scripture into these two languages) render "you received" in Psalm 68:18 as "you have given" and "you gave" respectively.

Another possibility is that Psalm 68 is itself based on Numbers 8 and 18. In this view, then, the Lord has taken the Levites (Numbers 8:6, 14) in order to give them back to the Israelites to minister on their behalf (Numbers 18:6). This would therefore fit well with the thoughts that follow in Ephesians 4:11-16. The reason Paul uses the word "gave" would be considered more explanatory with respect to the psalm than based on a different textual tradition or a misquote.[4]

Verse 9: There are at least three theories as to the nature of the descent mentioned in verse 9. One interpretation is that it refers to Christ's descent into the Hadean realm of the dead. In this view, Ephesians 4:9 connects with 1 Peter 3:19. The main problem with this interpretation seems to be that traditionally, "a descent into Hades is from the earth,"[5] but the descent and ascent in Ephesians 4:9-10 is to and from heaven.

A second major interpretation is that the descent refers to Jesus at his incarnation (and death). This arguably fits the "story" of Psalm 68, where God comes down from his holy mountain to win the victory, then ascends again.

[4] See P. T. O'Brien, "The Letter to the Ephesians" in *The Pillar New Testament Commentary*, gen. ed. D. A. Carson (Grand Rapids: Eerdmans, 1999), 292-293.
[5] O'Brien, 294.

Finally, there is the thought that the descent is of the Christ in the Spirit at Pentecost in Acts 2. The first problem with this theory is that Paul refers to an ascent following a descent, and the ascension followed by the descent of Acts 2 reverses the order. The second problem is that the account of Pentecost emphasizes the descent of the Spirit, not of Jesus.

On balance, the thought that the descent refers to Christ at his incarnation appears to be the best fit, but a case could be made for any of these views.

Verse 10: At some level, the exact descent to which Paul is referring does not really matter. We know Jesus came down or went down. The key point of the passage is that ultimately, Jesus ascended.

Jesus' ascent, as explained here by Paul, parallels several ideas already introduced in the letter. First, he ascended higher than "all the heavens," referring again to the multitiered heavens. We return to the Jesus enthroned in the heavenly realms far above all rule, authority, power and dominion (Ephesians 1:21).

Paul also tells us that Jesus ascended "in order to fill the whole universe." This parallels the idea of Ephesians 1:23 ("fills everything in every way") and refers to the lordship of Jesus. Paul does not appear to be saying that Jesus is going to fill up the universe in some physical or spiritual way. The word "fill" may well be an Old Testament allusion to Jeremiah 23:24 ("'Do not I fill heaven and earth?' declares the Lord"), referring to the lordship of Jesus.[6]

Verse 17: The Greek word translated as "futility" (*mataiotes*) expresses significant hollowness. In addition to futility, it can mean emptiness, purposelessness and transitoriness.[7] In the Septuagint (LXX), the original Greek translation of the Old Testament, the word is found often in Ecclesiastes.

Verse 19: The Greek verb rendered as "having lost all sensitivity" (*apalgeo*) can refer to skin so callused that it no longer feels

[6] O'Brien, 296-7.
[7] BAGD, 495.

pain. In the moral/ethical arena it means to "lose the capacity to feel shame or embarrassment."[8] The verb tense that Paul uses here—the perfect tense—describes something that began in the past and is continuing in action and/or effect in the present. Certainly one effect that ongoing sin has on us is to dull our sensitivity to conscience.

Verse 20: Time and again, Paul returns to the theme of spiritual understanding. In Ephesians 1:18ff he prays for the eyes of our heart to be enlightened; in Ephesians 3:17-19 he prays that we would understand the love of Christ. Paul's attitude seems to be that his readers do not need to know more about what to do, nor do they need to know more about Christ. They simply need to know Christ, which will take care of all their other needs. Here, Paul reminds the readers why they became Christians and establishes the driving motivation for all the "practicals" of Christian life that he is about to detail.

Verse 26: This verse opens up the possibility of being angry without sinning. Since Jesus apparently did just that in John 2:12-17 and elsewhere, it must be theoretically possible for anyone. In reality, however, it is difficult to distinguish between my righteous indignation and your ill temper! Another way to view this is to see anger as a natural reaction in certain situations and one that is not always sinful. However, when we are angry, the temptation to sin is very great, and reliance on God is needed to handle anger righteously. So, anger itself may not be sin, but what we do with it is the important issue.

Verse 28: The Greek word translated "work" (*kopiao*) means to toil to the point of weariness. It can refer to "mental or spiritual exertion."[9] It's the same word Paul uses in 1 Corinthians 15:10 to describe the effect of grace on his life.

Chapter Five

Verses 1-2: Imitation was the primary means of training in the Greek world. As usual, Paul gives us not only the charge

---

[8] O'Brien, 322.
[9] BAGD, 443.

("be imitators of God"), but also the motivation ("as dearly loved children").

Verse 3: The word translated "hint" in the New International Version is from the Greek verb *onomazo*, which means "to name" or to "use a name or word."[10] In other words, there should not even be a discussion of sexual immorality among disciples. Obviously, this does not mean we should not warn about or preach against sexual immorality or any other form of sin. It does mean, however, that we need to be very careful about how we talk about sin. Verse 4, warning against "obscenity, foolish talk or coarse joking," helps to underscore the point. Having said that we must emphasize that Paul's concern here really goes beyond how we talk about sin. It would seem like he is stating that fornication is to be considered so sinful and evil and contrary to the character of God as to be "unspeakable" behavior for us as God's children and imitators.

Verses 13-14: Paul, like most New Testament writers, uses the images of light and darkness in moral terms. The overall context of verses 8-14 seems to be the movement from darkness to the light. First, Paul talks about his readers having come from darkness to light; then he talks about the power of the light. Although some scholars suggest that verses 13-14a deal more with restoring Christians who are in sin, the overall thrust of thought seems to be that by our lives, we expose the life of darkness for what it is and can influence people to change. The J. B. Phillips rendering of verse 14a is, "It is even possible for light to turn the thing it shines upon into light also." (After all, it happened to you!)

Verse 14b has several possibilities as to its source. Several commentators lean toward Old Testament texts such as Isaiah 26:19 ("You who dwell in the dust, wake up and shout for joy!"), Isaiah 60:1 ("Arise, shine, for your light has come, and the glory of the Lord rises upon you") and Jonah 1:6 ("How can you sleep? Get up and call on your god!")[11]

[10] BAGD, 573-4.
[11] O'Brien, 374.

Although there are several possible links between these passages (especially in Isaiah) and verse 14b, "the dominant scholarly view claims that the original setting of the Ephesians hymn was a baptismal one."[12]

Verses 15-17: The wise disciple recognizes that he lives in evil days and must therefore be motivated to make the most of every opportunity. The parallel between verses 15 and 17 shows that to be wise is to understand the Lord's will. Paul has already taken great pains to show us that as disciples we have already escaped these evil days and are seated with Christ in the heavenly realms. Now we must take every opportunity to display ourselves as different from the world around us, both for the sake of one another (vv18-21) and for the sake of the lost (1 Timothy 2:3-5). In this way, we can remain faithful to the end and bring as many as possible with us.

Verses 18-21: These verses carry a double admonition. First, in verse 18a, there is a warning against drinking too much wine. Then, in verses 18b-21 Paul charges his readers to be filled with the Spirit and goes on to elaborate on that thought. Although verses 18-24 are partitioned into eight sentences in the New International Version, what they translate happens to be one long sentence in the original language. The original sentence has a series of dependent participle clauses, which would read:

> But be filled by the Spirit,
>> *speaking* to one another
>>> with psalms, hymns and spiritual songs,
>> *singing* and *making music* with your hearts to the
>>> Lord,
>> *giving thanks* to God
>>> for all things
>>> in the name of our Lord Jesus Christ,
>> *submitting* yourselves to one another
>>> in the fear of Christ,
>>> wives to husbands...[13]

[12] O'Brien, 376.
[13] O'Brien, 386-7.

Verse 21: With the author's permission, I will here give an alternative way to look at this passage. Much has been made of the word "submit" in this passage. The Greek word *hupotasso* means to subordinate or to subject someone or something. For example, it is the verb employed by Paul in Ephesians 1:22 to describe Christ's supremacy in the heavenly realms. In Ephesians 5:21, Paul uses the verb in what is called the middle voice, which would translate "submit yourself." In all of its New Testament appearances, the verb is used to indicate a specific ordering.

There is little to suggest that Paul is trying to describe a mutual submission. First, it might be argued that the verb does not really allow it. Second, while it might be argued that the term "one another" implies mutual submission, it is my contention that it does not necessarily demand it. There are many obvious instances where allelon is used to describe mutual action (e.g. Ephesians 4:25); but there are others that likely do not mean some sort of reciprocal action. For example, the admonition in Galatians 6:2 to "carry each other's burdens" does not mean that we exchange loads with one another. It means that those who have the capacity to help the weaker members need to do so.

In light of this, I believe Ephesians 5:21 serves as a topic sentence for Ephesians 5:22-6:9, in which we are called to be submissive to one another: wives to husbands, children to parents and slaves to masters. Any idea of reciprocity that Paul may intend will be developed in those verses. This does not preclude the need of the husband to lovingly serve his wife. However, Paul will use different terminology (e.g. "just as Christ loved the church") to communicate this.

Verses 26-27: There are at least two possibilities as to the meaning of Paul's reference, "washing with water through the word." One possibility is that the washing refers to baptism and the purification from sin that is available through Jesus. Another likely possibility is that the passage refers to the prenuptial bath God gave the nation of Israel in Ezekiel 16:8-14. The washing through the word would be the saving power of the gospel, as in

John 15:3 when Jesus said, "You are already clean because of the word I have spoken to you."

Chapter Six

Verse 4: It's probably worth noting that although children are called to obey both of their parents, it is the fathers who are called to special responsibility for parenting the children. In context of the times, this probably relates to the Roman *patria potestas*, which gave the father full authority over the child — technically even to the point of death — for the child's entire life. It is possible that "fathers" is a synecdoche for "fathers and mothers," especially since honoring "father and mother" was just mentioned.

For our purposes, we see the choice of either making our children angry (the more literal translation of the word rendered "exasperate") or bringing them up in the training and instruction of the Lord. Paul's concern is not simply that children obey their parents, but that ultimately they will come to know and obey God through their relationships with their parents. The old saying, "Your life is the first gospel your friends will ever read" could also be worded as "Your life is the first gospel your children will ever read."

Verse 10: Paul does not stop reminding us of our need to rely on God. He writes in what is known as the passive voice and is really admonishing us to "be strengthened." In other words, we will not fight and win the spiritual battle on the basis of strength that we acquire, but rather on the basis of strength given to us by God himself.

Verse 12: When Paul writes about our struggle, the word he uses (*pale*) carries the meaning of a wrestling match, which was a popular first century sport. In terms of the battle we fight against Satan, we are reminded that the weaponry is not a set of long-range missiles. Rather, the fighting is daily, hand-to-hand combat.

Verses 14-18: In his famous passage on the spiritual battle, Paul draws heavily on Old Testament imagery, especially from the book of Isaiah. He also appears to have in mind the equipment of the Roman legionnaire, with which most of his audience would have been familiar. Remember, Paul wrote this while in prison in Rome. He was possibly chained directly to a guard and did not need to simply imagine the armor as he wrote about it.

The belt of truth probably comes from the Septuagint version of Isaiah 11:4-5, which says: "With righteousness shall he be girded around his waist, and with truth bound around his sides." In terms of the armor of the Roman legionnaire, Paul probably pictures the leather girdle that protected the soldier's sides.

The breastplate of righteousness and helmet of salvation are found in Isaiah 59:17: "He put on righteousness as his breastplate, and the helmet of salvation on his head." The breastplate, of course, covered the chest of the soldier and thus guarded his heart. The righteousness that Paul has in mind may be our ethical righteousness (doing what is right), or perhaps he has Christ himself in mind. We put on Christ as our righteousness in baptism.

When Paul talks about the shield of faith, he is not referring to the small, round shield that soldiers sometimes carried. Rather, the shield he talks about measured four feet by two feet and was called the scutum. Soldiers often dipped them in water in order to ward off flaming arrows in battle.

The Old Testament reference for the "sword of the Spirit" is not as obvious as the others. He may have in mind Isaiah 11:4-5, which says: "He will strike the earth with the rod of his mouth; and with the breath of his lips he will slay the wicked." Regardless of the reference, the picture is striking. Paul does not refer to the long Roman broad sword. He refers to the short-handled sword used for close-in fighting — just the thing for the type of battle we face.

Prayer obviously holds a special place in the armor of God. The apostle uses "all" four times ("all occasions...all kinds... always...all the saints) in two short sentences (v18). Paul's admonishment to "be alert" may have in mind the challenge we face in staying focused as we pray — remember the apostles in the garden. He may also have in mind the idea of perseverance until the end (Jesus' Parable of the Ten Virgins in Matthew 25).

Whose armor is this, anyway? Obviously on one level this is the armor supplied by God to the saints. However, the Old Testament describes this as the armor that God himself wears into battle. Indeed we could reasonably picture God giving us his own personal armor so that we might experience the same type of victory over Satan and his minions which he enjoys. Finally, if instead of the belt, breastplate and shield, we think of putting on truth, righteousness, faith, salvation, etc., then we could say that to put on the armor of God is to clothe ourselves with God himself. Paul may be thinking of Ephesians 5:1, where we are commanded to imitate God. The more we fight to become like Jesus, the more we will experience spiritual victory.

Who Are We?

Discipleship Publications International (DPI) began publishing in 1993. We are a nonprofit Christian publisher affiliated with the International Churches of Christ, committed to publishing and distributing materials that honor God, lift up Jesus Christ and show how his message practically applies to all areas of life. We have a deep conviction that no one changes life like Jesus and that the implementation of his teaching will revolutionize any life, any marriage, any family and any singles household.

Since our beginning, we have published more than 100 titles; plus, we have produced a number of important, spiritual audio products. More than one million volumes have been printed, and our works have been translated into more than a dozen languages — international is not just a part of our name! Our books are shipped regularly to every inhabited continent.

To see a more detailed description of our works, find us on the World Wide Web at www.dpibooks.org. You can order books by calling 1-888-DPI-BOOK twenty-four hours a day.

We appreciate the hundreds of comments we have received from readers. We would love to hear from you. Here are other ways to get in touch:

Mail: DPI, 2 Sterling Road, Billerica, MA 01862-2595
E-Mail: dpibooks@icoc.org

Find Us on the World Wide Web

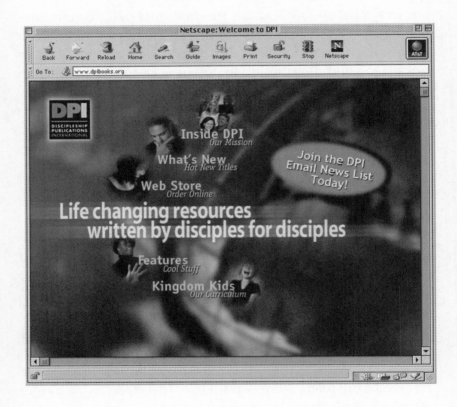

www.dpibooks.org
1-888-DPI-BOOK